Praise for *The 1*

From someone who has lived the li̇   ̇, ᴛ, ᴛʜɪꜱ ɪꜱ a well written book. I have faced the possibility of something going terribly wrong every time I stepped foot on the deck of a boat. She has described what went on in a way fishermen know and those who have never commercial fished will understand. This old salt enjoyed it greatly!

> Larry Ryser
> *Deadliest Catch, FV Incentive* deck boss;
> Kodiak Queen captain

Calkin has written a fascinating book about an intriguing search and rescue case that took place off the coast in the Pacific Northwest. Although written decades after the fact, the particulars of this case remain very vivid in my mind. I distinctly recall debriefing the helicopter pilots and crew and observing their excitement in locating and finally rescuing the skipper of the F/V Fargo. While the book is from the fisherman's point of view, she did an excellent job of detailing the Coast Guard's perspective of the case. Filled with poignant moments and good detail, it is an outstanding read and one that I highly recommend.

> Rear Admiral Dave Kunkel
> U. S. Coast Guard (retired)

If ever we needed a story on the triumph of the human spirit and one man's ability to reinvent himself, this is it. *The Night Orion Fell* will never leave me, and for good reason. It's a great story, carefully researched, and compellingly told. Bravo Abigail Calkin.

> Kim Heacox
> The Only Kayak and Visions of a Wild America

The Night Orion Fell tells a hard story in careful detail, full of Oregon, of courageous people and Larry Hills, one stubborn, lucky sonofabitch. You won't walk the docks past a trawler next time without wincing.

> Jon Broderick
> Setnetter, Fisherpoet

In the spirit of Sebastian Junger, author Abigail Calkin clinically and beautifully explores the unforgettable and tragic true story of the 1982 fishing disaster off the Pacific Coast. Calkin's retelling is one of remarkable hope and resilience. A powerful story.

Christopher Robbins, CEO, Gibbs Smith

Writing with necessary precision and extraordinary imaginative power, Abigail B. Calkin tells the compelling, true story of a freak accident on a North Pacific trawler. One man, died, one survived. The machinery of a trawler is the stuff of nightmares, but Calkin tells the story with such empathy and careful attention to detail that the result is not merely horrifying but a most moving and humane account, both of the accident itself and of its long-term consequences. I am grateful for an in-depth portrait of an astonishingly brave man, and also of a tight-knit community, the fishermen, Coast Guard and their families along the Oregon coast. At a time when public life is so mired in greed and dishonesty, this book presents the sort of unassuming courage, endurance, and co-operation that can still make one feel proud of the human species.

David M. Black
Why Things Matter

A fine, fine piece of writing. Calkin obviously did an incredible amount of research for such accuracy and detail. Her sketches of both fishermen and Coast Guardsmen add to the depth of the story.

Francis E. Caldwell
Land of the Ocean Mist and Pacific Troller

THE NIGHT
ORION
FELL

Also by Abigail B. Calkin

Nonfiction

Pebbles, Mops, and Thimigs (1974)

Eating with a Spoon (1975)

Toilet Training: Help for the Delayed Learner (1978)

Performance Enhancement Training:
Change Your Thoughts, Feelings, & Urges,
(First edition) (2009)

Fiction

Nikolin (1994)

The Carolyne Letters (1995)

THE NIGHT ORION FELL
A SURVIVAL STORY

Abigail B. Calkin

Copyright © 2012 by Abigail B. Calkin
www.abigailcalkin.com
www.fernhillpress.com

All rights reserved

Printed in the United States of America

First printing 2012

Library of Congress Cataloging-in-Publication Data
ISBN 978-0-6155-9193-3

Calkin, Abigail B.
    The night orion fell: A survival story/Abigail B. Calkin
    ISBN 978-0-6155-9193-3
    1 Commercial Fishing 2. Survival 3. United States Coast Guard
    4. U. S. Forest Service 5. Oregon 6. Abigail B. Calkin 7. Nonfiction

Copy Editor: Marcia K. Malott
Cover design: Laura Van Tine
Author photograph: Sean Neilson

Part I and a segment of Part II previously published by Scroll Press at
http://www.scrollinspace.com, 2008

To
Larry, Bev & Lincoln Hills,
whose lives were forever altered

To
Ray Shultz, John Whiddon, Gary Ellis, Mike Moore, Dave Glenn,
Mike Wood, John Lutz, George MacGillis, William Clayton,
David Vandecoevering, and Fred Hamann,
and the others involved in the rescue

In memory of
Dick Cooley
&
those we know
who have died at sea

The sea is a primal magnet, and maybe theirs were journeys into mystery and wilderness.
Linda Hogan

The sea is impersonal. Every year it eats people and goes on not caring.
Lincoln Hills

The vast immortal sea shall have her own.
Depoe Bay, Oregon marker

The sea abides and takes its due when she chooses. I never want to be a token in that payback again.
Larry Hills

TABLE OF CONTENTS

PROLOGUE

As you read this tale, you will encounter heroes. None of them meant to be a hero—it just happened to them. For the most part they were just doing their duty. Duty to a service, duty to shipmates, duty to family, duty to friends, duty to themselves, and in the process they became heroes.

Some of them, over time, came to wear that cape with pride, some wear it lightly, and some wear it like a shroud. However they wear it, for a few hours of concentrated time they all had it thrown over their shoulders without realizing it or acknowledging it as they did their duty as the intensity of the moment dictated without hesitation. Oh yes, they were afraid—only a fool wouldn't be—but they did their duty with tight guts and wide eyes to try and save another human being the only way possible, by putting their own life and limb on the line.

As you read this tale, you will encounter heroes—people pulled out of everyday ordinary life and thrust into extraordinary circumstances. Some came through unscathed, others slightly scathed, others scathed for life, others dead. All of the living will never forget those moments.

Larry Hills, 2009

AUTHOR'S COMMENT

I met Larry Hills in May 2003. Through an ad in the county's only newspaper, the weekly Lake County Examiner, I called Beverly Hills to wallpaper a room in my husband's childhood home that we now own. I had turned my sister-in-law's room into my study and bought some cloth wall covering that was two shades of soft rose pink. My husband said it would make the room look like a French whorehouse while Bev admired its fine quality.

Other than realizing I had hired an expert, the first day was routine and business-like; the second day began as routine for me. For Bev, it was more—she knew I was an author and she looked at the titles and topics of my wall of books. True, she didn't see any books on commercial fishing or the ocean, but her thoughts verged from calculating their family budget and how much she'd make on this job to my writing. Bev papered and I continued to sort the drawers of the antique secretary my mother had left me. Inside were her diary and memorabilia from when she lived in Paris, love letters my father wrote her, carved whalebone crochet hooks from my Nova Scotian grandmother's youth in the seafaring town of Lunenburg. I fingered the smoothness of one of Mary Isabella Acker's crochet hooks as I read my mother's diary then went upstairs to ask Bev if she wanted something to drink. How serendipitous it seemed when a few months later I learned that my grandmother's father and brother had died in separate incidents at sea when she was still a child.

"No thanks," she said, then blurted out "I go home to fix my husband's lunch. He's disabled from a commercial fishing accident and he works for the Forest Service now." She continued with a couple of quick details of the accident her husband, Larry, had had 20 years earlier—his deckhand was killed and Larry hung in the trawl lines on deck for two days until the Coast Guard found him. The non sequitur was seamless to her, but I had not had the privilege of getting from her finances to my bookshelves to her husband's accident. I listened politely, expressed my horror, then went downstairs to continue perusing my family's past. Instead, I returned to those tasks with the detachment of a file clerk. Forty-five minutes later I realized I'd thought of nothing but Larry's story and had separated it into incidents and chapters.

PART I

THE ACCIDENT

We are free to choose but not

free from the consequences

that follow that choice.

Christopher Robbins

As the lines continued winding over the portside gunwale and onto the drum, Larry heard a short, gut-launched scream. He whirled around to see Dick's feet going over the top of the net reel. Part of the line lashed Dick ever more tightly in its mechanical turn as it rolled over him and rolled him over the reel. In that instant, Larry saw Dick's terror-stricken face, pallid and frozen. His adrenalin surged and although he considered the longer, safer route around the net reel, he instinctively took the shortest route racing over the incoming line to shut off the hydraulic motor. Putting his hand on top of the core of the net reel, he boosted himself across the starboard hose line, something he'd done countless times before…although never while the lines were moving nor while wearing his heavy foul weather gear. With its normal wear on even one haul, the line had developed indentations and small frays that snagged first his gloved right fingers and wrist, then took hold and whipped up his arm. It pulled him over the line and slammed him face down against the net reel, his arms flung out as he reached to rescue Dick. Over the noise of the boat and its hydraulics and on his own first revolution, Larry heard Dick's bones snap as the line wrapped and crushed him in its vise. The steel hose line cudgeled down Larry's left arm, jolting and jerking him repeatedly. Fastened to the reel, Larry spun in continuous revolutions, feet over head, head over feet, again and again. The force flung his hat, boots and a sock God knows where.

The lines had now whipped and wrapped the two men against the reel like captured fish. Only the wind and Dick heard Larry's cold words:

"We're dead."

As soon as his feet left the deck, Larry thought this thing's gonna grind us up. He visioned himself and Dick as mush. Innards out in the air. Two lives mulched into the beyond.

One cross of the line against his torso would break and crush his bones as easily as it had just done Dick's. The wings and body of the net ground over the gunwale and across the deck toward the reel. Within a minute or two, its slow, steady, unstoppable pace would pull tons of fish on board. In moments, the weight and webbing of the net would bring to bear the final pressure needed to kill Larry and Dick.

If only the net'll fall over the flange on that side of the winch.... If it'll just fall over that flange, it'll jam up that roller bearing. I've seen it happen. The motor won't turn the reel. It'll jam it 'cause it can't break that hose line inside the gear.

A skilled skipper maneuvers his boat to roll the hose lines and net evenly onto the reel. Wrapped against it, Larry could not steer. The line began to wind unevenly and drag toward the edge of the spool. It wedged over the drum's flange and onto the chain and gear sprocket to catch in the bearing, jamming the hydraulic motor, preventing it from turning the drum. When the drum stopped, the trawl doors were still drawn against the sides of the boat, hanging unfastened from the gallows posts. Larry hung upside down suspended facing the reel, bowed against its under-side, his back toward the deck, arms spread eagle, his feet not far from the stern and not quite touching the deck. Motionless and trapped, he listened to the prop wash of water against the stern, the drag of the net webbing, and the hydraulics screak of a siren's call.

He called out, "Dick. You OK?"

PART II

TRAWLING

Loneliness is but a speck on the

human condition of isolation.

Beth Hovind

Garibaldi is a small, quiet northwest Oregon town nestled between coastal mountains and Tillamook Bay. For centuries it had been a Tillamook Native whaling village. By 1880 the tribe had so few members it ceased to exist. In the 1970s and 1980s, Garibaldi became one of 12 major fishing ports between San Francisco and the Canadian border. In 1982, it was a community of 1,000 people whose livelihood depended on commercial fishing and lumber shipping. Dick Cooley had grown up in Garibaldi, went through the school with several of the Vandecoeverings, a commercial fishing family, and now had a wife and two young boys. Larry Hills was a newcomer from the Willamette Valley, married one of the Vandecoevering girls 10 years earlier, and had become a part of the fishing business. As with any business, commercial fishing depended on the whims of nature. Some years were good, others spare.

Storm followed storm the fall and winter of 1981-1982 and brought little opportunity to cross the Garibaldi Bar between Tillamook Bay and the ocean. When the fishermen did go out, weather bound them to fish only one or two days at a time. Thursday, Feb. 4 dawned clear. Larry always spent his wife's birthday, Feb. 6, in port, but this season it was critical to go fishing the first clear five-day stretch. That morning on his way down to the boat, Larry stopped by the hardware store for a couple of bolts for the stabilizers as well as some new hacksaw blades for the trip. Contrary to the superstition against leaving on a Friday, he planned a night departure on the 11:00 high tide, Friday, Feb. 5, confident he and his deck hands, Dan Fisher and Dick Cooley, would have good fishing.

Dan was a slight, soft-spoken fellow of average height. His mannerisms didn't give away much of who he was, but every now and then he'd talk with his hands or nod a few times as he smiled. Larry was a contrast in every way. Standing 6' 4," he had reddish hair, a red beard, and was very comfortable with words. He was kind and intelligent. He joked a lot with people, which had a way of putting them at ease quickly.

Early in the afternoon, Dan, his intended first mate, called to say he had cut his hand badly on a broken glass when doing the dishes. He'd been to the hospital to get stitches, but unable to use the injured hand he could not go. *That's not good,* Larry thought. *Dan's a hard worker. Good boat experience and he knows what to do without me telling him. He's been a deckhand for me on the Fargo a number of times before, and last fall spent a month helping me convert this from a double-rigged shrimper to a single-rigged trawler.*

Larry and Dan had removed the shrimping outriggers and built deck grates to cover the back deck work area. A crane lifted the net reel system off the dock and swung it into place on the back deck. They bolted its 5-foot tall white stanchions to the back of the stern deck. Its two A-frames supported the flanges. The stanchions and the huge bolts that fastened the 10-foot long net reel to them had been painted white in September's boat preparation. They also rotated the main winches 90 degrees to pull from the stern instead of from abeam with the outriggers as they did when shrimping. What Larry with all his familiarity with his equipment had never noticed was how similar the individual parts looked to a set of medieval torture instruments. Stanchions to hang someone from. A flange or net reel to spin someone on. Doors to fasten a person to before dipping them repeatedly into the ocean. No, Larry's thoughts now and previously had always focused on the beauty and efficiency of the *F/V Fargo*. She floated white with black trim and was a sweetheart of a vessel whether a shrimper or a trawler.

Already on the boat for the trawl season, the green net with its attached floats was carefully rolled on the reel from the last time Larry and Dan went out trawling. Framing the ends of the net reel itself, about 10 feet apart, were the flanges, huge round disks, also painted white. When empty of its net, the steel drum looked much like a bare giant spool for thread or electric cable line. Larry could see over the top of the reel and as he backed away to do a quick visual scan of the work, he also admired the vessel. The doors rested against the deck, tightly fastened to the gallows posts. P*aint job's holding up well,* he thought as he imagined the noises of trawling: the chains lift the doors, the trawl wheel grinds the net out to sea, the winches pull it up from the ocean floor. He smiled as he anticipated these noises of the trip and good fishing.

Dan and Larry also installed improved deck lighting because they knew winter fishing involved working a lot at night. They mounted a high-volume water pump on board for washing the mud out of the fish tow. Then, except for five or six one-day trips when it wasn't storming, they, like other fishermen up and down the coast, waited for the weather to clear.

Larry knew he'd miss Dan's experience on the trip.

That's OK, not great but OK, thought Larry. *Dick's not trawled before, but he spent two months tuna fishing with David off southern California last summer. That brother-in-law of mine always has the best luck—walks away from car accidents, was a skipper before he could legally buy beer, has one of the biggest and nicest boats in the fleet. Then he finished another two months with another brother-in-law, Dave Jordan, and both said Dick was great.*

Larry thought about the times, before he'd married David's sister, the two of them had gone to bars together and Larry had watched him walk up to a girl, give his charmed smile, introduce himself and flat-out ask her how she liked him so far. Any young woman would smile at him, step a little closer, while Larry stood shyly by observing his smooth and winning manner. On the ocean, the fish seem to swim into his nets. Ever since they worked on the *Miss Lorraine* together in 1973 and 1974, Larry always thought of David as a kid brother more than as a brother-in-law. He knew he still held a grudging respect for David's catching abilities.

David says Dick's good, but with only the two of us on board, that leaves no spare minute for a long conversation or good read, or even a decent sleep, but we'll be OK.

As usual before a trip, Bev and Larry went upstairs for a long nap, essential to a fisherman before his days of little to no sleep. Their son, Lincoln, wouldn't be home from school till mid afternoon. She was upset he was not going to be home for her 30th birthday. *Damn!* she thought, *I might as well be married to a soldier who's always going off to some war. I have no control here and he expects me to be sweet and kind and understanding. And to say 'Bye, Honey. I love you. Be safe and come home to us. I'll keep everything perfect.'* Sarcasm riddled her unspoken words.

"I'll be here for the next one, honey, I promise. It'll be OK. This has been a really bad year. We need any money! We can't afford me not going out for this whole window of good weather." She was not persuaded. She wiped away the sarcasm but not the half-pout.

"You'll miss the race tomorrow with Tony. I know you can beat him from here to Rockaway. That's $100."

A couple of months earlier at a family gathering, Larry and his brother-in-law, Tony Vandecoevering, also a commercial fisherman, got into an argument even they considered silly: Who could run faster? They wagered $100, a pricey sum in a winter of poor fishing and little income, on a footrace across the five-mile sandy beach from Garibaldi to Rockaway, jetty to jetty. With much bravado, Larry offered, "I'll even run the last quarter mile backward and still beat you!" Tony, 22, thought he could beat this 34-year-old man, but almost daily all that winter, Larry put on some large, heavy logging boots to run the hard-sand route. His plan was to run the distance, barefoot, light-footed. The two scheduled the race for Saturday, Feb. 6, Bev's birthday. When Bev's birthday came, Larry and Tony were out fishing and each knew he could beat the other. Larry knew he would make hundreds of dollars on this trip, much more than their silly wager. Grandiose challenge or not, Larry was in fine physical condition as he prepared to depart on this trip. To this day, he and Tony still josh about who would have won.

He viewed this discussion with Bev as silly as the wager, ending it saying, "I'm going fishing tonight. And right now, I'd rather make love with you than argue."

As Larry dozed off afterward, he ruminated on two-manning the trip. *David said Dick was a solid fellow, would make a good deck hand. We'll be OK,* kept running through his mind as he lay with his arm curled around Bev. She, nursing her disappointment almost into anger, had trouble falling asleep.

After a leisurely dinner, Bev did the dishes, smiling while she listened to Larry and their 7-year-old son, Lincoln, wrestle on the living room floor. She dried her hands, then leaned against the doorjamb to watch. Larry tucked Lincoln under one arm and ran in circles around the living room, Lincoln yelping with delight. In a quick dash, Larry took the stairs two at a time and dropped his son onto the bed. Lincoln announced amidst his bounces of laughter, "When I grow up, I'm going fishing with you."

"And right now, you're going to sleep!" said Larry as he tugged the sheets up under Lincoln's chin with a resolve that told the boy that talk was finished till he returned from the fishing trip. Bev arrived, her tender smile still present, and sat down to give Lincoln his goodnight kiss.

As she and Larry walked downstairs, she admonished him, "Oh, he'll take forever to go to sleep, he's so wound up."

"Aw, he'll go to sleep happy," he slipped his arms around her, "and then I'll wind you up."

"Not before I finish packing your food," she said, slipping away, once again upset he planned to leave the day before her birthday.

Bev returned to the kitchen and scanned the box: peanut butter and jam, cheese and crackers, bacon, onions, potatoes, and coffee. She topped it off with two loaves of bread she'd made that morning and two dozen eggs.

Oh, where did I hide those cookies I made, she schemed, casting a glance his direction to be sure he wasn't looking. He wasn't. She placed them under the small package of Oreo cookies he liked so much. Larry packed a change of clothes into a duffel bag, then turned to the box on the counter by the door to add extra flashlight batteries, several pairs of gloves, and the two packages of new hacksaw blades. His old ones were pretty dull and he never knew when he'd need them. He thought of having run into his brother-in-law, David, that morning at the hardware store. David had said, "Dick's really excited to be going out with you." Larry smiled as he and Bev loaded the boxes into the back of the pickup. All this was routine to her. Her father had started commercial fishing before she started school. Her brothers became fishermen when they were teenagers. The girls married fishermen, and the Vandecoevering commercial interests grew to become one of the largest family-owned fishing fleets on the Pacific Coast. Once established, Bev's parents, Larry and Lorraine Vandecoevering, also went into the charter business, first purchasing the Solo, the last wooden boat the Coast Guard certified as a passenger boat. The family continued to add more charter boats and restaurant businesses.

Larry looked at the clock. 8:30 p.m. He'd told Dick to meet him at the *Fargo* at 9:45 p.m. Plenty of time. He followed Bev upstairs to their bedroom before his departure. As he got up to shower, he ran his fingers through her hair and kissed her on the forehead, offering, "Happy birthday. Have a good tomorrow."

"Lincoln and I'll go to Mom and Dad's."

He took her hands in his, storing their feel and softness in his memory. She felt his calluses, the roughness of the fisherman's hands she knew so well, and smelled the sweet diesel and the organic odor of the ocean that had permeated her growing up and now resided throughout her home.

"Time to go."

"Yes. Time." She spoke flatly, burying her disappointment and worries before they fully surfaced. She stood and brushed her hair as she watched him dress, waited at the bedroom balcony door while he went to kiss a sleeping Lincoln. When he came back, he took her in his arms and after one last, long kiss, he walked out the side door onto the small deck and the stairs his youngest brother-in-law, George, had just built for them. Slick as everything was with frost, he felt the smoothness of the well-planed rails. He liked having that outdoor access from the bedroom, he thought as he descended the stairs and climbed into his pickup for the five-minute drive to the dock. To leave his bedroom for a fishing trip was his idea of perfection. Bev waited for the sound of the engine starting up, then closed her eyes almost reflexively as she heard it. She walked out on the deck and watched him pull out, turn down the hill of Seventh Street, cross Highway 101, and drive past her parents' restaurant, The Troller. His headlights disappeared then reappeared before finally going behind Joe's Charters. She stood in the chilly air, shivering, knowing he would be pulling his blue 1980 International Harvester Scout pickup in front of her parents' old red storage building.

How many trips has he captained the *Fargo?* At least 50, Bev thought in her usual and unconscious wife's way to say he'd come back from this trip too. Although she usually didn't hide her emotions, she buried the thought that this was his first captaining of the Fargo on a midwinter two-man trawling trip. Larry wasn't concerned, though, for he had midwinter trawled under other captains, maybe 80 times, across three years and had certainly captained any number of shrimping or trawling trips on the *Fargo*.

Missing him already, she wiped the tears off her cheeks and dashed back inside, rubbing her arms rapidly. Crawling back into bed, she snuggled her face into his pillow, and with the ken of a fisherman's daughter, sister, and wife, she mentally watched his actions at the dock and on the boat as she fell asleep.

Larry gathered a load from the pickup bed and crossed the street to the narrow way that led to the dock and the *Fargo*. He felt that usual elation—life is replete—as he walked between Joe's Charters and Smith's Pacific Shrimp Co. Smith's owners, the Schreibers, also owned the *Fargo* and Larry always tied up alongside the company dock. Good-looking boat, he thought as he recollected his first sight of her 13 years earlier when, built by Fred Larson from North Dakota, she had just been launched and was running down Newport's Yaquina Bay for her sea trials. He was on the deck of the *Ruby,* deck handing for the boat owner, his childhood friend, John Rice, as the *Fargo* put out to sea. That image of her held in his mind. Brand spanking new, he found her impressive as hell. A big boat for that time was 55 to 65 feet and the Fargo was 52 feet. Her distinctive flying bridge and attitude in the water had impressed Larry as he viewed her from the deck of the 32-foot wooden troller, *Ruby.*

Eagerly anticipating his first trawling trip, Dick had already kissed his two sleeping boys, Joey his six-year-old stepson whose father had died when he was a year old, and Billy, his two-year-old son, said goodbye to his wife and father as he left. He arrived 15 minutes early. He stood on the dock studying, admiring the *Fargo* until he saw Larry's headlights go past The Troller. He walked back to where he knew Larry parked, ready to help carry gear. On the long tuna trip as a deck hand for David Vandecoevering, the sea bug had bitten him and he was eager for any job on a boat. An unobtrusive yet likable 29-year-old local, he was a quiet, open-faced fellow with a sincere mien and, Larry noted, honest eyes. He stood about 5' 9" and slender. He had the same shoulder length straight hair he'd had in high school and now had a scruffy, thin beard as well. He wore a gray sweatshirt, rain pants, and rubber boots. He seemed just one of the ordinary fellows hanging around the docks looking for work. Different from many, however, Dick was unpretentious, the kind of guy a skipper wants for a deck hand. He didn't brag about dragging up everything from sperm whales to Dover sole on his way to the Aleutians, only to grow clueless when told to tie or release a bowline. Although he didn't know him well, Larry could tell as they loaded, he would like having Dick on board.

"No hair hanging out, Dick. It could get caught in the machinery," Larry stated, also noticing Dick had already cut his sweatshirt sleeves off at the elbows, another of Larry's safety rules around unforgiving machinery.

Dick looked at Larry's short hair and neatly trimmed short beard as he tucked his shoulder-length, straight hair into the standard blue knit cap. Larry had already told him about his firm rule of no alcohol allowed while at sea on any vessel he skippered. Once, to cut the pain caused by breaking his wrist the day before a trip, he took four shots of apricot brandy while towing. He towed into a current running perpendicular to his course. He felt too calm and behaved too slowly. Before he could react, he had crossed his gear tangling both nets and all four doors. The trip ended immediately because he had to go in to repair his gear. He vowed he'd never drink on board again, nor would he allow it. Trawling with its heavy machinery and complex maneuvers doesn't mix well with alcohol.

Dick helped Larry carry and arrange the food and gear, both of them cautious on the thin-iced street, dock, and deck. Dick followed his directions to the letter. Larry put the survival suits in the unused head below with a stash of tools, including his hacksaw and blades.

He checked the pressure-release life raft atop the wheelhouse. Secure. The logbook, in which every 15 minutes he'd record his LORAN readings, location, and heading, and his navigational chart lay handy for quick access next to the compass on the counter behind his captain's chair. Down in the engine room, he rechecked his fuel levels. His saddle tanks had 200 gallons each plus he had two tanks full — 1,500 gallons of diesel each—more than enough for this four- to five-day trip. The 50-gallon lube oil tank was full. The two banks of batteries, one on either side of the engine room, were fully charged. He went up to the wheelhouse and started the Wood Freeman autopilot. Anyone who spends time at the dock knows the sound of each sea boat: FV Fargo was getting ready to go out. Larry readied himself for this five-day, two-man trip during which he and Dick would work 24 hours a day with brief snatches for sleep and food. He scanned the instruments—radar, three radios, chromoscope, and depth finder, LORAN—all on and working. After working on the Ike the winter before, and becoming accustomed to a chromoscope, he had to have one. He smiled at it. Not everyone had one of these great colored depth finders that showed with such fantastic clarity the details of the ocean floor with its hills, valleys, sunken ships, and schools of fish. His VHF would keep him in touch with his buddies. Garibaldi fishermen had set up codes that gave them a way to share information about where to fish without broadcasting it to everyone with a VHF radio. The VHF was every fisherman's lifeline for making money and, if necessary, saving someone's life or boat. His single sideband he rarely used, but sometimes he listened even as faraway as Alaska.

The *Fargo,* now fully loaded, including eight tons of ice for fish preservation, and with gear stowed, was ready. Larry walked up to the flying bridge. It was cold but at least it wasn't going to rain on him. Dick untied the lines and Larry reversed the engine to back the *Fargo* out the 200 feet to the neck of the channel. Turning to port, he backed north till he had enough clearance to turn toward the bay before he headed to the bar and ocean beyond.

From the flying bridge, Larry thought again, almost without realizing it, how he would two-man this trip. Although he didn't want thoughts of Bev to interfere at this moment, he couldn't help it. It had not been a great evening at home with him about to miss her birthday. He really did need to spend more time with his family. Picking out the buoys with his spotlight, that stupid big marine light never had worked well, he headed the Fargo down the bay at 5 knots. Looking back, he scanned the deck—all secure—and watched his new deck hand, Dick, out for his first trawling trip. He was checking the net reel, winch, and lines, all the while smelling fish and diesel, smells Larry no longer thought about but just accepted as a comfort of his world.

Moving out feels good, thought Larry as the 5-knot breeze blew against him. The *Fargo* had just passed the rock abutments. Moving along the north shore, he sped up to 10 knots when, turning back to steer, he inadvertently tangled the cord around his ankle and pulled the spotlight off the bridge's binnacle board. The sealed beam lens shattered as it landed on the steel deck of the flying bridge.

"Aw, damn!" he muttered to himself. "Broke my spotlight."

Leaving on a Friday and Dan having cut his hand, the broken light portended Larry's third omen. Superstition be damned, he didn't believe in it anyway, especially in this lean year. Any one of these events might have caused another not to go out or to turn back. Some fishermen took with them all the spiritual and superstitious behaviors they could muster…anything to help, God forbid they should need it…to survive and avoid the abyssal depth.

To go out on the vast sea, even if the next boat is a quarter mile away, a fisherman needs extra protection. He has his practical things— radio, life raft, survival suits. But he needs to take more—his omens and religion. David, Larry's brother-in-law, admits he is superstitious, won't go out on a Friday, and now with Larry's accident followed two years later to the week by his youngest brother George's capsize and death, won't go out in Februarys. Such omens vary from seaport to seaport, family to family. No whistling on the boat. Don't take a woman on board. Never leave port on a Friday. Don't say "banana" or "rabbit" while on board, but touch lead if you do. How do these men, so brawny, courageous, tough, and practical, come to believe such omens? Much can go wrong at sea and sometimes no amount of strength or grit makes a spit of difference. Storms roll in; rogue waves swamp the deck; ice builds up, sinks the ship without a trace; windows in the wheelhouse break; men wash overboard never to be seen again. In a vain attempt to control the uncontrollable and not be a victim, fishermen assign imaginary connections between events, and give false causation to their safety.

A woman on board may distract the crew, although it is known that captains as recently as the 1800s occasionally took their families with them. Not going out on Fridays started with respect for the crucifixion and spread throughout Christian societies. Go out fishing but never on a Friday, the boat has no problems, the catch is good, and the fisherman comes home safely—that is his reward. The superstition about Fridays becomes a charm and its 2,000-year history strengthens.

No, Larry wasn't superstitious. Nor did he think the Higher Power would save him if he got in trouble. That was his responsibility. He would be cautious and careful. Common sense and safety were his watchwords on any fishing trip.

Larry continued toward the bar, and the solitude of ocean, time, and planet, that solitude he found so fulfilling. Crossing at flood tide tonight—and no reason was ever good enough to make Larry cross the Garibaldi Bar on its dangerous ebb—the half-mile wide bar was one of its calmer masses of whirls and swells. He responded to the familiar small pitches without thought as he steered. Carefully, now with only the mast light and the light of the clear night, he continued to move between the markers till he viewed the seas as they changed from bay to open ocean. A few moments later, savoring the solitude he relished, he turned to face the cold, east wind for a last view of the comfort of home and harbor. He saw the smallness of himself on the grand scale of the ocean that lay before him.

Glad it's no colder than it is…. Rime ice on everything. But not quite cold enough to ice up. Jeez, it's flat as a lake out here. Still. Calm. This is as close to perfect as it's gonna get for winter fishing. The boat held so steady on the sea, no engine parts or trawl gear clanked. He felt only the hum of the engine in his feet.

As he continued south to the grounds he often fished, Bev's disappointment and his guilt at leaving before her birthday nipped again like a mosquito at the edges of his thoughts. He poured himself a cup of coffee from the thermos and continued his heading toward Cape Meares. In the middle of the night, coffee was his main staple until its edge drove him to the galley after a peanut butter and jelly sandwich. He let Dick steer for those few minutes.

The National Fisherman, oceanographic and other fishing magazines upright in the rack at the end of the table caught his eye. Unlike most fishing vessels, the *Fargo* had no girlie magazines on board. The first time Larry brought one home, a few months into married life, was the last one he bought. Bev hit the ceiling and said, "My father doesn't have them on his boats or in his house. You're not going to either." She never asked for much control in the marriage so what little she requested, or demanded, he gave her. Not much of an issue for him because his stepfather had never had them around either, it was just a new habit he'd learned from some of the boats he'd worked on. Anyway, he loved to read about the science of the ocean when he took a break.

Not many breaks on this shorthanded trip, he thought.

He found the homemade cookies in the box Bev had packed and felt even guiltier about having left on Friday. It was after midnight now. Her birthday!

"Aw jeez, Bev, happy birthday!" he said to the blue denim wallpaper she had put in the galley early in the fall to cover the food, grease, and coffee stains on the paneling. It really was a pretty posh setup for a fishing vessel with the denim here and Gibson Girl wallpaper in his stateroom. He smiled as he pictured her papering the galley.

One September day after the owners of the *Fargo* asked Larry to captain the boat, Bev informed him she was going to do a bit more than muck it out—she was going to paper the galley and stateroom. OK, thought Larry, this boat is really filthy, even for a fisherman. As for Larry's stateroom, an inch short of the 6' 4" he needed merely for his height, it was covered in a paneling that had turned black from filth.

Bev had started hanging paper before she started school. Her mother and aunts all had papered their houses and Bev tagged along to various homes helping and learning. By 1980, she opened her own business in Tillamook County, Beverly Hills Wallpapering. She silently pooh-poohed her brother David's laughing at her desire to paper the *Fargo*. Everyone in the family knew that Bev was a nut for any series of projects. She'd already done a room in every family member's home and at least 24 other places in Tillamook County, often doing entire houses. The family just shook their heads at her latest turn. Give her a surface and she'd come up with a way to cover it.

It was a warm day when they arrived at the *Fargo,* Bev with a bucket of materials—cleaning supplies, rolls of paper, paste, brush—and Bullet, their basset hound, following her. Larry understood the denim choice for the galley—plain and manly, but was baffled by her choice of Gibson Girl what with everyone in her family involved in commercial fishing. Bev's thinking was self-serving: He'd get his pinups but in her style. Her reply was simple: It was on sale and the cheapest in the store. He had smiled then as he smiled now. He'd married the right woman. She kept her eye on the dollar.

On the one hand, this job looked easy—she wasn't papering Victorian homes with 12- or 14-foot ceilings. On the other hand, she had to consider that the boat had one angle when level, but plugged to capacity after good hauls, it could list. She would have to hang the paper so it wouldn't be at a tilt when level or listed. She was meticulous as she scrubbed the walls in preparation for improvement. Taking on the "she" of the boat, she spent a half-day scrubbing the galley wall behind the stove and small sink free of its years of grease on grease layers. Disgusting, she thought, about to put up the denim paper. It will look much better when I'm done and give these fellows a couple moments of pleasure as they pour a cup of coffee, scramble up a Scootin'-'Long-the-Shore, or make a peanut butter and jelly sandwich.

By noon, she had finished cleaning the galley walls and they would be dry enough to start papering in an hour or so. Larry smiled at her as she unpacked his favorite lunch—sandwiches on homemade bread, dill pickles she'd made last month, and oatmeal raisin cookies. Her brown, wavy hair was a little unkempt from the morning, but she looked dang cute in those yellow shorts. He admired her figure and long legs. Yep, she's a keeper. When he came in for a cup of coffee midafternoon, she stood with her hands on her hips admiring the galley's walls. "Looking good!" he said, not specifying whether he meant the galley or his wife. She silently accepted both compliments.

As she worked, she thought about the day she first met Larry in 1970, about 100 feet from where the *Fargo* tied up. He and another man sat on the gunwale of the *Teddy Jo*. The man listened to Larry talk about Shakespeare and archeology, the subjects that had interested him most in college. He wore a lavender shirt, a blue bandana tied around his neck, and his cap set on his head at a jaunty angle. She looked at his gorgeous red beard, beautiful blue eyes and forgot why she came down to the dock. He smiled at her and she smiled back.

"You still burning the toast?"

"What? I never burned any customer's toast."

"You burned mine yesterday when you served me breakfast."

"No, I did not," and love and a lifetime relationship began.

Nine years later, like the amulet a medieval lady tied to her knight's arm, the she of this wife was doing everything she could to protect the she of her husband's boat. She stepped back to admire her work, the unbeknownst talisman to the vessel's safety. Meanwhile, Larry was on the back deck rigging for shrimping or in the engine room cleaning, checking, or repairing something.

The next morning, she examined the walls in his stateroom. Six-foot strips made this an easy job. She'd grown up in Garibaldi with parents in the fishing business, had gone to school with most of the local fishermen, waited on them at her parents' restaurant, The Troller, and was well known in town for her perky personality. One and all fishermen down at the dock came by to kid her over wallpapering the *Fargo*. When she finished at the end of the third day, she stepped back to check her work. Laugh away, Fishermen! This looks really nice, she thought.

Laugh away was what one of the Coast Guardsmen and his wife would do years later when they learned Bev had wallpapered the *Fargo*. Mike had been a commercial fisherman as well as a Coastie. On hearing of the wallpaper, Mike and Peggy Wood simultaneously blurted a guffaw of astonishment.

Back in the wheelhouse and checking his LORAN again—he'd been in the galley less than 10 minutes—Larry saw a school swimming onto the edge of his chromascope screen. About to set his first trawl two hours south of the Garibaldi Bar off Cape Meares, he changed his speed to slow ahead and throttled back the engine to 500 rpm. He and Dick donned their oilskins and thigh-high Uniroyal boots. Grabbing his Helly Hansen jacket off its hook behind the captain's chair, Larry put it on as he went out on deck. It didn't matter that it wasn't raining; the spray would make it wet out there. He explained to Dick what was about to happen when they set the gear. When they let out the elongated conical net, first to hit the water would be the cod end that narrows to a closure where the catch accumulates, followed by the long tapering belly that holds the fish, the broad mouth that scoops the fish, and finally the wings at the front that provide an opening wide enough to catch some entire schools. The steel doors are five by eight feet and weigh 1,000 pounds each and hold the net's mouth open during dragging. Attached to the net on one end and the doors on the other is the hose gear. This hose gear is comprised of flexible steel cable wrapped in hydraulic hose with steel wire mesh sheathing. These cable lines fasten to the mammoth steel doors. Dick repeated all this to himself, amazed that Larry seemed to know in the dark when all these parts would leave the boat and be in the water. "Do it enough," Larry told him, "And you dream about letting out the net and bringing it back in. It's a rhythmic thing."

Larry started to reverse the net reel's hydraulic motor to begin putting the trawl net into the sea. He never turned over the net release to any deck hand on his first trawling trip and would not turn over control of the hydraulics for hauling in until the middle of the second day, midday Sunday. This meant that the trip was slower and more arduous for Larry as he ran back and forth from the wheelhouse correcting the steering to the back deck to control and monitor the net as it slid into the water. Larry worked the port side and hydraulics and Dick the starboard side. During the release of the net, Dick became less aware of the vibration of the boat and the smell of diesel as he concentrated on the net rolling into the ocean.

When Larry returned to the wheelhouse to guide the boat, he switched on the tow lights atop the mast. The tow and the deck lights, visible for miles, burned in the darkness. The tow lights let other vessels know not to cut too close and that he has limited maneuverability. Larry ran back and forth between the back deck and the wheelhouse. As they lowered the doors with the two main winches, Larry manned one winch, Dick the other. The doors woofed into the sea, gliding, spreading the net as the forward motion of the boat pushed the water to pressure the doors apart to the 58-foot spread of the net's mouth. Even. Balanced. The gear was set. Larry upped the throttle and the gear moved out, responding to the pull of the tension of the net and steel doors. From the forward motion of the vessel, the net gradually assumed its funnel shape. Eye still on the chromoscope and the LORAN, hand on the autopilot control knob, Larry steered the Fargo while the net glided slowly along the bottom of the ocean floor scooping up every fish that swam in front of its mouth, keeping anything with a diameter bigger than 4 inches.

"OK, Dick. We're gonna start hauling," he announced after about 30 minutes. He switched on the autopilot to run ahead into the swell then throttled back at one-quarter speed, and nodded as he heard the engine revs go down. Each man at one main winch, they maneuvered the doors onto the gallows posts as they came up. They disconnected the doors from the main towing cables and attached the hose line lines to the net reel. With the reel winding, both sides continued to pull evenly, as the gear wound up to the bridles that connected the top and bottom of each wing of the net, Larry in control of the net reel winch this first day.

Two wraps of the steel cable came up soon and lay evenly across the net reel as the wings emerged from the water.

The net was too heavy. He should see it and some floats by now, but it hung straight down out of sight.

The wings came up further, wound on evenly, followed by the body, the intermediate portion, of the net. Finally, the cod end began to emerge.

"Fucking dog sharks!" Larry announced before the net reached the surface. These small sharks form large, dense schools at the bottom. They weigh heavy, can easily poke a gloved hand with their spines, and have no market value. Their schools are dense and therefore, if the net does not wind on evenly, it may jam in the hydraulics. This slows the whole trawling operation down since the only remedy is to let the net out and start rewinding it again. Once he had turned the *Fargo* and lifted the net with the boom winches, Larry leaned out and released the bell at the cod end. Most of the dog sharks fell back into the ocean, but those that lined the sides of the net got their heads and sharp gills stuck in every mesh. Larry and Dick labored to hand release these now-dead fish, grabbing each head one by one, squeezing it, and with a jerk of a wrist snapped each fish out of the net's mesh. After that waste of a good hour, Larry wound the net onto the drum.

He looked up to stare at the starred heavens and smiled. It felt good out here on the vast ocean, good to be fishing, damned dog sharks and all. Now, net on the reel, and doors on the gallows posts fastened and chained one to the other high across the deck with the boom winch, he headed farther south, letting Dick steer for the first long stretch while he studied the chart to plan his next few sets. Had Dan been along, Larry would already have his next set planned and would be catching some sleep while Dan steered.

Larry went to the galley to make another pot of coffee. As it brewed, he opened Oceans, a research magazine, and read about five pages before the pot gave off its familiar noise that said the coffee was ready. The steady, deep, growling hum of the Caterpillar engine still sounded so right, it passed unnoticed, just what he wanted.

By Sunday morning near dawn, they were setting the fifth trawl off Haystack Rock near Pacific City. So it continued. They had a few tons of rockfish and rex sole in the hold but nothing to smile about. Tow after tow, day after day, Larry and Dick hauled up mostly dog sharks.

Larry radioed other fishermen. Gil Fletcher on the *Freedom's Lady* was doing OK fishing with about 600 fathoms of towing cable line out. Bev's brother, David, was out but just offshore, in deep water and hauling in also. The *Fargo,* however, was only rigged for midlevel trawling with 750 fathoms of cable line so could only bottom fish in waters of 250 fathoms.

When Sunday's daylight broke, they were near Neskowin, offshore of Two Arches—halfway between Pacific City and Lincoln City to its south. Larry told Dick to head southwest to a reading that was due west of Lincoln City in 75 fathoms of water, then wake him when they got there. He was going to get an hour's sleep. This would be his second sleep of the trip; the first one had been those two hours stolen early Saturday evening. Concerned his worry about slim catches would keep him awake, Larry had had no coffee for about six hours and had just fixed each of them a fried egg sandwich. A satisfied stomach and no coffee surely would make him sleep. For an hour, Larry sat in the wheelhouse watching Dick monitor the electronics and standing wheel watch. Comfortable he was doing a good job, Larry then went to his bunk. He lay in his stateroom staring at Bev's wallpaper, pissed as hell he couldn't fall asleep.

"Larry! Larry!" Dick was shaking him awake. "Larry!"

Short on rest and in the middle of a deep sleep, Larry was not ready to wake up. He was confused for a second. Oh that hallucinatory drunk nature of exhaustion from much work and no sleep that started quietly and blurred his thoughts. Suddenly, remembering he held full responsibility for the safety and success of the trip and the money they earned…or didn't, he bolted to standing, now wide-awake.

"We're there. West of Lincoln City."

"OK! Let's set the gear."

As the net went out, the noises—the hydraulic winch, the reel unwinding, the engine—were so familiar and right to Larry, he did not consciously hear any of them. What he heard were the cries of the approaching gulls. He looked around—a small group of puffins floated nearby. What fat, funny birds they were, their wings too short for their bodies.

"Here you go, Skipper." Dick handed him a cup of coffee. "You been fishing since you were a kid?"

Larry glanced at him. "Thanks. I suppose you could say that. I used to take my pole and slip off to the creeks around Salem when I should have been mowing the yard or cleaning my room. Got a few whippings from my mom, stepdad, or granddad for that but trading one for one, every fish was worth it!

"Good coffee, Dick. I was a pretty normal kid growing up in the Valley. After I graduated from high school I went to college in Monmouth and later to Portland State, majored in English, took a lot of anthropology—loved that and my Shakespeare class." He went on to describe Monmouth, a town that hasn't changed in a hundred years, quaint and quiet with even a working blacksmith shop on the main street. From there he went over to Newport the summer of '69 to work on his friend John Rice's commercial fishing boat and fell in love with fishing. He never went back to college. It was the allure of being able to do something alone and in a place where the rules are few but absolute that attracted him.

"Your folks divorced?" Dick asked coming back to Larry's mention of his step-dad.

"No. My dad was killed in Korea. I was 3."

"Bummer. That must be hard, not knowing your father."

"I don't think much about it. No options. All my mom's tears and my wishes didn't bring him back. But when I was 5, I looked in the drawer where she kept the newspaper. It was at the top of the front page. State capital but my dad's picture was on the top of the front page. The first thing my mom heard me read aloud was that obituary from the Salem paper. Net's towing fine. You can go catch a half hour if you want."

"Nah, I'm fine. Clear. But no fog," Dick said, angling his head as if that would help him understand better Larry's sudden and skillful change in topic.

"No, that east wind blowing off the Coastal Range will keep the fog from forming," Larry explained, still wanting to avoid talking about his father.

"What kinds of things you done in fishing?"

"Lots. The weirdest one was just last winter. It was blowing about 40. We were on the *Ike* and the hold had about 12 tons in it. That boat could haul 110,000 pounds with the hold absolutely plugged and nothing on deck.

"One time, we came into Astoria like that and threw ourselves in our bunks while we waited for the plant to open. Some guy came running into the galley and woke us all up with shouts we were sinking. We told him to shut the fuck up, we were just plugged.

"Anyway this time in that 40-knot wind, we were hauling back such a big tow of rockfish, about 70,000 pounds, we had to bring it on by thirds too. We had put a third of the fish on deck in the deck checker bins when the middle bin broke. All the fish on deck slid to the port gunwales. That threw the boat off balance and caused the fish in the hold to slide too. Next thing we knew, we were at 45 degrees looking like we were about to capsize. Our port stern quarter was totally submerged and still getting slammed by waves in those gale-force winds. Leo Kuntz, the skipper, and probably the best trawl fisherman I've ever been associated with, hollered for me to get my survival suit on.

"'Want yours?' I hollered back.

"'Hell yes!' His eyes were as big as the bottom of a Navy coffee mug.

"Right then I knew we were in trouble; Leo was hard to rattle when it came to seamanship. Not a guy to call the Coast Guard on some piddley-ass thing, but I knew he had this time. I put mine on and threw his up the pilothouse stairwell to him.

"He asked who wanted to go out to cut the net to release the load we'd just brought up. I volunteered quicker than Mickey so I walked out on top of that net full of fish as it floated about 6-foot wide on the surface, knife in hand—walking on water!—sat down in the middle of the net and started cutting. Broke the blade. Leo tossed me another knife. You know what it's like trying to catch a knife coming flying at you through the gale-force winds with those survival suit mitts? I grabbed it in my arms, didn't cut my suit, and started cutting again. Got six more feet cut and then that knife slid out of my mitts it was so slippery with fish scales and slime. Leo tossed me a third knife! This one was his own personal one, the one he always carried in the sheath on his belt. He had to unzip his survival suit to get to it. The whole time I cut on the net, the water was sloshing that tubular cod end in the surge of seas that were also coming on board. I kept glancing over at the port stabilizer pole, which was pointing straight down, on one of my looks. Aw shit! I want that to be parallel to the water, not vertical in it! I wanted to keep cutting until I started to see that set of aluminum poles start to go past vertical, because that meant she was on her way over and I had seconds to get myself as far away from the boat and net as I could. I could have looked at the boat, but you get tunnel vision when you're in an emergency 'cause you gotta stay focused on your portion of that. Gotta stay blind to everything else. The stabilizer poles, the struts, were my only indicator of the attitude of the Ike for a long time. Meanwhile, Leo was pumping the chilled seawater coolant off the fish hold. Mick did what he could to shift the weight of the fish on deck. Still straddling the cod end that moved with the surges of water, I finally got a hole in the net big enough for the fish to start floating out of the gash. It was then the stabilizer struts started slowly, slowly climbing back up. Ever so slowly that boat started righting itself. That's when I knew we'd be riding that tough, green, pit bull of a boat back to Astoria.

"We canceled the Coast Guard call but it was nip and tuck. I'm convinced if the Ike hadn't been a whaleback design with watertight hatches on the deck and house, we'd have been swimming for it.

"The strangest part of that whole thing was going to get my foul weather gear back on. There, behind my winch, I had folded and neatly stacked my damn gear. Who in his right mind would *fold* his gear when the boat was listing at 45 degrees? I must have been a monk with some inner sense of calm about to be hanged for a heretic!"

Larry threw back his head and gave a roar of a laugh.

"You *folded* your gear?" Dick asked in amazement.

"Yeah, can you imagine? I was scared shitless, yet folded my gear up nice and neat!

"Another time I worked on the *Dennis Gayle* out of Eureka. We fished regularly at 5,000 feet, that's about 830 fathoms. We'd bring up huge catches of fish from untouched grounds. But things were really weird down there and we had to use special thick-walled floats on the net. Trawling at those depths, we brought up some strange looking sea life. A lot of things are totally exploded and they're just all…all the fish with swim bladders come up with these swim bladders sticking out of their mouths because of the decompression of bringing the stuff up. In fact, on those boats, those deep water Dover-sole boats, it sometimes takes 45 minutes just to wind the gear up, that long for those big drums just to wind it, because you always have to put out anywhere from two to three times as much cable line just to reach the bottom, so you're putting out a couple of miles of cable.

"Sometimes we even brought up fumaroles. Now those are strange looking things. Short funnels that sit on the floor of the ocean. They grow into stalagmites of all kinds of heights, a yellow mass of mushrooming looking things that comes up from the bottom. Break through the earth's crust to cool really quickly in the chill of deep ocean waters. Formations that break off and end up in the net when we're dragging that deep."

Fumaroles are thermal vents openings that also occur on dry land. Near ancient or present volcanic activity, these openings are usually in areas where the magma is shallow enough to escape through the earth's crust. It is the combination of minerals and gasses that form these fumaroles. Such were some of the contents of the *Dennis Gayle's* net when trawling a mile deep.

A couple of stories later, it was time to haul back again.

Out on deck in the dawn's sunlight and chill air, Dick operated the net reel winch and Larry steered, always looking back at the net to see if it was coming up evenly. Again, it did not float to the surface burgeoning with rockfish and mixed sole. Probably another load of those damn dog sharks! Kittiwakes and gulls were ready, soaring, plunging, flapping, crying, resting in the water. All watching. All waiting for the release of the dead dog sharks. Murres and guillemots floated on the wait. As Larry looked back at the net, he sighted shearwaters. Such a graceful bird, he thought, as he watched them glide a few feet above the water waiting for offal.

He turned to check his instruments.

Once again, Larry and Dick dumped their load of dog sharks.

"Well, Dick, we've run out of paper towels. Maybe we just ought to call it a trip and head back in."

Dick looked startled. "I just saw a roll in the galley."

Larry laughed. "Nah! That's the joke to go in when the fishing's gone to shit. Or we ran out of mustard."

Larry laughed and Dick smiled. He liked Larry's sense of humor and calm manner even when there was a lot to do.

With daylight breaking, Dick brewed a fresh pot of coffee, then cooked up some bacon, potatoes and onions, threw a few eggs on top, stirred the whole mess, added salt, pepper, and cayenne. It was still calm enough they could eat in the wheelhouse.

Sunday, Feb. 7, dawned still clear on land as well. At home, Bev threw a Pendleton mackinaw over her bathrobe as she went out for the Sunday Oregonian, Portland's paper read throughout the state. She stood there in the chill for a moment looking down at the bay and out to sea, at Venus in the west, and wondered what Larry was doing at that very moment.

Please bring him home to us. Plugged. We sure could use the money. Realizing she was chilled and the coffee was probably ready, she hurried inside.

At the kitchen table with her coffee, Lincoln still sound asleep, she pulled out the ads to read later, read the funnies then set them aside for Lincoln. Having read the first section, she turned to its Northwest Magazine.

On the front page was a photograph of the now-upright crabber, Sagacious, grounded and obviously damaged from its capsize. The headline read, "TRAGEDY STRIKES THE WEST COAST: At least 33 people have died in fishing-related accidents in recent months." She, the wife of a fisherman out with a green deck hand, did not need to see this. She already knew it was a deadly season. Every restaurant on the coast that ever served a cup of coffee to fishermen or Coasties knew this. You could see it on any face in the grocery store as locals gave a somber nod or wan smile to friends, avoided eye contact with the occasional stranger who traveled the road in winter. Must have money. Is he gonna make it back?

Turning to page 2, the lead article title, "The Grim Harvest in Fisherman's Lives," was not written with coastal families in mind. Portland lies 50 miles inland as the crow flies. Fishermen don't live in Portland. No. The cover with its headline and photo was designed for those who lived in the city, the Valley, the Cascades, or Eastern Oregon. Its message was: Be glad you're a rancher, a logger, or an office worker. Be glad your life isn't being harvested. It didn't mention until the fifth page of the article, that the four crew of the Sagacious were rescued.

As it turned out, between October 1981 and Feb. 7 1982 when the article was published, 33 fishermen from San Francisco to the Canadian border had died; more deaths were yet to come. This would become the deadliest season on the century's record.

As Bev read the *Sunday Oregonian,* her brother, David, was trawling deep water out off the entrance to Tillamook Bay. Her other two brothers, Tony and George, were trawling off Astoria, and Larry had just hauled up his net off Pacific City's Haystack Rock. All she knew was that her worry, just below the surface, was now about to explode. She tried to read the article. She tried not to read the article. She didn't see the words, but she did see names of boats and people she knew. A knot gripped her and she couldn't release it. She silently chanted over and over and over all that day and the next and the next, *everything will be fine. Everything will be fine.*

She had skipped over the name that caught every Oregon and Washington Coast Guardsman in the throat—Capt. Frank Olson, the CO of Station North Bend was killed during an attempted rescue mission when his helo malfunctioned and crashed in the ocean. Lt. j.g. Ray Shultz with his crew including flight mechanic, George MacGillis, was headed down from Station Astoria to rescue Olson and his crew but the southerly headwinds blew so fiercely, it took Shultz an hour to get the 20 miles to Seaside. Still having over 100 miles to go, he called Station Tillamook Bay, 40 miles farther south, and was told they'd just had a gust of 115 miles per hour. After this Marine-turned-Coast Guard pilot maneuvered the dicey but judicious turn back north, his helo was in Astoria in minutes. Years later, with a catch in his voice and turning his head away, Shultz described this turning back as the most difficult thing he'd ever done. A pilot doesn't leave a fellow pilot and his crew in the ocean...unless the rescue means losing his own life, crew, and helo. Fishermen and Coast Guardsmen knew this was the worst fall and winter they'd ever seen.

Although they had a few thousand pounds of mixed rex and Dover sole and rockfish on board, finding little else others than dog sharks by Tuesday and with the forecast predicting a strong storm front within 24 hours, Larry decided to call it an unsuccessful trip and head in. It had warmed and was a little above freezing, no ice on the deck now. The sky was still clear. He and Dick ran out the net, cleaned it, reeled it back in, stowed it, and called the cannery to say they were coming in that evening with a small load. Larry pulled off his industrial grade, midthigh Uniroyal boots and put on his deck boots, the knee-high ones.

As they headed north, two Dall porpoises moved and leapt alongside the Fargo. Larry smiled remembering the time he was shrimping the previous summer, and the motor suddenly quit while they were double-rigged, pulling two nets side by side while running north against a south-running current. He had yelled at his deck hand to watch which way they were drifting as he dove for the engine room. By the time Larry found the problem—a plugged filter, bled the injectors, and restarted the diesel engine, the deckhand realized he had not paid careful enough attention and could not tell Larry what direction they were going and if they had drifted over their gear. This was serious because Larry needed to turn in that direction in order not to foul the nets. What to do? On a hunch, he decided his best course was to follow the porpoises that had been with them all afternoon. After towing on the nets enough to pull everything back taut, they hauled back both nets and sets of doors without any tangled gear. What a touch of luck, he thought, to have those Dall porpoises right there!

What had then seemed a lucky hunch to Larry, though, is the skill of unconsciously noticing and remembering important events he may need later. The person most apt to survive a crisis is the aware one who, with the same clarity as he writes locations in his captain's logbook, marks important events that, unconsciously remembered, often turn out to be essential to survival.

That evening Larry looked at the house lights as they began to go off for the night, people comfortable in their beds. *What the hell am I doing bouncing around out here?* he wondered, and he looked forward to going in even though it was just a break-even trip. He had the Garibaldi whistle buoy in sight when he received a radio call from Fred on the *Willapa Maid*.

"Hey, I just got out here at the gas station. Got seven boxes."

Larry thought about that. A "box" was the code between Larry and Fred for a thousand pounds. Seven thousand pounds. He could salvage this trip with a haul like that. Although close to home, knowing those elongated sole had good market value and knowing the *Fargo* had far too few fish in the hold to call it a trip, Larry decided to head north to the "gas station," that large undersea formation of shale where Fred was. One good tow of rex would make this a successful trip and he could still get back to port on the next flood tide. Meanwhile, David and Gil were outside the shale pile fishing deep water for petrale sole.

A shallow entrance on the Garibaldi Bar means big surf—up to and over 20-foot waves or the keel can hit the sand in the shallows between waves. The entrance between the rocky breakwaters is narrow and there was always the possibility of a boat turning broadside and rolling. There is zero room for error. No. Larry knew he never wanted to cross on an ebb. He'd been on boats that did. One time, Uncle Kenny was coming in on the *Miss Lorraine* after a trip on which Larry and David were deck hands. The bar was rough enough that Kenny had them in the wheelhouse. This 72-foot vessel got slammed from behind by one of those breakers bigger than 20 feet. It came down as dead weight full on top of the wheelhouse with enough force to blow all the old paint out of the seams. The house instantly filled with a fine white mist of pulverized paint blasted from the wood seams. Knocked to his knees and the hell scared out of him, Larry vowed he'd never cross the Garibaldi Bar on the ebb when there was a big swell running.

As he turned from his approach to the Garibaldi Bar, he called the cannery, Hoy Bros. Fish Co. to say he was not coming in, but was going to make one more tow. He headed out to the shale pile 20 miles northwest of Neahkahnie Mountain. With renewed optimism and a smile on Dick's face, they set to work. The boat began to list slightly and, for balance, Larry switched from one of the big diesel tanks to the smaller saddle tank. The hydraulics hummed as the net rolled out. They unhooked the doors, and once off the gallows posts, Larry lowered them into the water, set them, and the main towlines headed toward the bottom 400 feet below. They trawled in pretty much a straight line to lay her down, right up a trough just off the north northwest tip of the shale, near where Fred had just gotten two big tows of rex sole and mixed rockfish. About 8:00 p.m. that Tuesday, Larry started hauling his net full of rex sole up from the bottom. Still headed northwest, he radioed Hoy Bros. Fish Co. again to tell them he'd be there on the next flood tide, daylight the next morning. Fred and his *Willapa Maid* were on their way in. David radioed to say, "We're almost done hauling and we'll be *right behind you.*"

Larry responded, "We're hauling back, and with any luck, we'll split and lift, and throw this tow on deck. Then we'll be right behind you."

He hung up the VHF receiver and once again, grabbed his Helly Hansens, pulled on the pants, thought about his Uniroyal boots but decided this would be a quick load they wouldn't sort, and slipped on his jacket. He walked toward the stern to bring on deck the last tow of the trip. The deck lights glared down from the boom and pilothouse to turn 9:00 p.m. into daylight. It was still clear and flat calm as their last tow wound up from the bottom. Larry winched first the port then the starboard doors up to their gallows posts and hooked the door chains into the eye of each door. Simultaneously, as they landed each door, Dick winched the tension off and each settled its weight onto the hook of its post. Larry decided to save the final fastening until the net was on board. With much to do right now, he preferred to keep an eye on the net and reel, correcting the steering as needed. The two men hooked the tail-chains from the doors to the net reel to begin winding the hose line in and to the drum. Dick, on the port side of the reel, once again operated the valve to roll the cable line up from the ocean and onto the drum. As usual with a two-person crew, Larry ran back and forth working the reel on deck then to the wheelhouse to steer the *Fargo* so the lines would wind evenly. When the net came up, he planned to set the catch on the deck and make a quick run to the harbor, home from a moneymaking trip just ahead of the predicted bad weather.

Lines almost fully in and wrapping around the reel, 20 to 30 feet behind the vessel the net wings and floats emerged into view against the surface of the black water. The deck lights glinted on the tops of the swells and against the wet, steel-embedded hose that covered the cable line. Larry turned to head back to the wheelhouse to right the steering a small bit.

PART III

THE NIGHT ORION FELL

Alone, alone, all, all alone

Alone on a wide wide sea.

Samuel Taylor Coleridge,

The Rime of the Ancient Mariner

Chapter 1

"Dick! Dick!

"Dick!"

It was then Larry realized Dick was dead. He hung there shocked, stunned. Oppressed with guilt, repulsed by the dead body next to him, and guilty for feeling that repulsion, he hung gripped in a stranglehold as tight as the cables that bound him.

Before his eyes flashed an image of Dick's boys, his 2-and-a-half-year-old son, Billy, and his stepson, Joey, age 6. Larry saw his own son, Lincoln, with them. He watched as the three young boys played together, then the image stopped mid-scene and vanished in a millisecond. In the next 40 hours, this intelligent, educated man would think any possible thought he could, except one: When he was three, his father was killed in Korea, almost 31 years ago to the day. In his effort to stay alive he erased the image of the little boys playing. He could not consider how his loss cemented his refusal to die, his refusal to leave Bev and Lincoln.

What a honeymoon! Hawaii was great, wasn't it? The Oregon Desert—trapping, bucking hay bales, walking. Riding my red tricycle. Mom's beautiful voice as she played the piano. Ah shit, I see the terror on your face, Dick. It's a strobe light and the flashing images keep repeating faster than you flipping in the net. Piss on Reaganomics! Drove me out of business at the Honker Outdoor Store. Lakeview—might not be in this fix but for that. A dense, black fear crept into his pores and he hollered at it, "Fuck you! Get the goddamn fuck out of here!" He saw old girlfriends and old cars. He thought of Dick's old girlfriends and cars. On and on and on.

But he didn't think of his father. Oh no. His father meant he could die also. Leave Bev. Leave Lincoln. Leave his mother too, losing him to the profession she hated his having. He could not think that Dick's boys had lost their father, suddenly and just like he had as a boy. Billy about the same age too. No, he couldn't afford those thoughts and the guilt that would shroud him.

He didn't connect his father's death to his own life and entrapment. First Lt. L. Bruce Hills was called back to active duty four and a half years after World War II where he had served in seven Pacific locations. Arriving in Korea in October 1950, he led a rear guard for the Eighth Army's withdrawal from the Chinese assault, guarded a mountain pass, wrote letters home December 12, January 13, and was killed February 13. Today was February 9. No, Larry could not afford to think of his father or Dick's boys. He didn't hear his mother playing and singing "Onward Christian Soldiers" over and over, breaking down, sobbing as she played. He saw only his own stubbornness and will to survive. *By damn! Fuck it! I'm gonna make it.*

Briefly, he tilted his head to see an upside down view of Neahkahnie Mountain backlit by the stars. The net, containing tons of rex sole and Dover sole, hung over the stern of the *Fargo*. Jammed, the hydraulic motor had stopped rotating, as the noise of that mechanical monster changed to a sustained ear-piercing screak. The false daylight from the deck lights scorched down on the net reel and the men it held but did not change the darkness that lay beyond the edges of the stern.

From the wheelhouse, the radio crackled to life.

"*Fargo, Fargo*. This is the *Cindy Lou II*. We're heading in. Where are you?" David hailed the *Fargo* multiple times with no response, then wondered why his brother-in-law had started for port without telling him. Again, the radio blared into the now-empty wheelhouse, calling to the coffee cups, pans, the skillet, and books that lay about.

Raising his head, Larry saw the lights and shape of the *Cindy Lou II* move slowly by. David was headed in and, busy on deck, he and his crew probably aware they were passing someone's vessel in the dark, did not attend to any particulars but their own.

"David! DAVID!" he screamed and yelled, but how could anyone hear him even a quarter mile distant over the sound of the diesel engines and the trawl gears of both vessels? Larry watched helplessly as David's boat disappeared into the black of night. His heart sank as he watched the lights vanish in the direction of Garibaldi Harbor. He felt his testicles move up into his body, safe from the reality that bred fear.

Suspended in time, Larry hung in stunned inactivity for a few more minutes...until his anger kicked in and he found he was damn pissed off.

I dodged this thing. This cable line didn't kill me. I'm not bleeding badly. Things aren't going to get a whole lot worse...at least not now. The net reel jammed and it probably isn't gonna turn. Gotta get rid of this chew 'cause I sure as hell don't want to swallow it.

Aw shit.

There's no damn way out short of being rescued.

There's gotta be a way out. There's always a way out. I dodged the cable line. There's gotta be a way out.

His fury spurred him to a rapid review of options. He pulled hard and long, trying to rip off his left arm. If he succeeded, he could reach the hydraulic valve with a leg, kick it into reverse, and get out of this thing, dash to the pilothouse where he could then stick his stump of an arm on the diesel stove to cauterize it. Put a tourniquet on it. Radio the Coast Guard. Maybe if he ripped off his arm.... He pulled, pulled till, nauseous and dizzy, he almost blacked out from pain. Passing out he knew he didn't want—too easy to slip from there to death. Death. No! Lincoln would grow up without a dad to take him fishing, camping, to teach him.... He tried pulling again but felt bile in his throat this time. He tried chewing his way out—cheek and jaw against his shoulder, he chomped the hose covered cable line and broke a couple of teeth.

OK. OK. I'm not getting out of here short of rescue. Gotta keep warm. Gotta keep the blood moving down my veins. Gotta keep the blood going to my hands. Gotta keep the blood going. Gotta keep the circulation going in my arms. They're pinched. Damn, they're tight. Strangled. They hurt worse than Hell. Keep the blood moving. Keep the blood moving!

Larry consciously worked to keep the blood flowing through his arms, knowing instinctively that to relax meant to lose both of them. He tightened them, gently pulling, tensing and relaxing them in spite of the pain. He visualized his blood flowing down his arteries, back up his veins...all night long. He refused to allow himself to fall asleep, knowing that sleep meant death. His mixture of rationality and anger, combined with the effects of his father's death, succored him.

As David pulled into the Garibaldi docks in the wee hours of Wednesday morning, he looked at the empty *Fargo* slip, then scanned the other harbor docks and slips for Larry's boat. Nowhere. When he didn't see the *Fargo*, an uneasy niggling settled in his shoulders. He called the *Fargo* again. He called Hoy Bros. They reported Larry had called to say he was on his way in. Yeah, he was a little overdue. David contacted other fishermen just in or on their way.

He called one last time before heading home to sleep, dirt tired from his trip.

"Calling *Fargo*. *Fargo*. Come in. Come in Larry."

"Larry are you on? Dick are you out there?"

Elsewhere in town, David's and Bev's sister, Marge Vandecoevering Jordan, finished the dishes after she had put her year-old son down for the night. She had married Dave Jordan, a fellow from California who came into port at Garibaldi one day, liked it, stayed, met and married Marge, one of the five Vandecoevering girls. She listened to Channel 16 on the VHF as others might listen to background music or the TV — not hearing anything till something caught her ear. David talked to Fred, Gil talked to David, Fred talked to someone at Smith's Pacific Shrimp Co. The idle but comforting chatter filled the silent worry about her husband, brothers, brother-in-law, and friends out there on the unforgiving sea. Suddenly, she realized she had heard the voices of all the other men but no one from the *Fargo* had responded for a good hour. She stared at the VHF, fastened to the bottom of an upper kitchen cabinet, as if that would produce Larry or Dick's voice. Their continued absence gripped this fisherman's wife with the fear of something gone wrong at sea.

I'm not meant to die like this. I dodged that cable. I'm not meant to die like this. Out here. All alone. Strung up. He remained both desperate and powerless to answer the calls.

He slipped into the summer of 1965, sweating in the dry, Oregon heat of mid-90 degree temperatures as he drove tractor and laid irrigation lines for the ZX, one of the largest ranches in the country. He drifted to archeology thinking about how he loved his amateur work in Oregon's High Desert, that north end of the Great Basin, which stretches on down to the Mexican border, and lies full of remnants of Native life from 12,000 years ago. He moved to the summer of 1968, exempt from the draft as the only surviving son of a war casualty. Away from college for the summer, he commercial fished out of Newport. Fell in love with Bev. Married her. For six months they continued their honeymoon on the ZX as Larry worked. Under the stars of this cold February night, he wended back and forth between commercial fishing and life in the desert of Lake County. He fished out of Tillamook Bay. He packed up and drove back to the desert with Bev and 6-month-old Lincoln. He trapped for beaver and muskrat and anything else worth the price of their skin, worked for the ZX again. Guided visitors, patrolled for vandals, livestock and property thieves, and managed wild game. He earned in a month on the ranch what he had earned in a day's fishing. *Better than being strung up against this fucking net reel.* He went to Garibaldi again in 1980 to commercial fish.

He careened through time and it slowed until each instant, each excruciating agony reached out and touched him again. Nothing existed but time, pain, and shivering in the cold. Again, he visualized warm blood flowing down his arms, into his hands, and back up through his wrists, past his elbows and muscles, back to his heart. Warm blood. It flowed, and he watched his will pull it back to his heart, cleanse it, push it down again to his hands and fingers.

Dark seconds lengthened to hours as the *Fargo* idled farther and farther offshore running at about 3 knots into the long slow ocean swells that came from the distant, approaching storm front.

In the dark morning hours, he let his head hang back, looked at the stars in their familiar positions. The Big Dipper and Cassiopeia sparkled. His eyes focused on Orion, his favorite constellation, and specifically Betelgeuse. He filled in from memory the stars he could not see. Familiarity provided only split seconds of comfort before Orion began to quiver as if it were a person on his side falling into the sea. Here, here! he called out. He had to remain conscious or he would die. He focused on Betelgeuse, concentrated until he could feel its heat warm him. When Betelgeuse no longer gave sufficient warmth, he picked another of Orion's stars and concentrated on the power of its heat flowing through him. As dawn came nearer, Orion's left arm and leg and part of the belt gradually sank into the sea. Finally his right arm and leg also disappeared.

Larry had spent many days in the early and mid-70s trekking in the solitude of the desert. Checking and setting traps. The days of getting muskrats were over and more recently it had been beaver. As he approached one trap, he saw from a distance that he had something. Another beaver. Releasing it, he saw scratch marks from the teeth and claws on the metal but gave them little thought. He had not heard its growls or screeches before it died. He had not watched its desperate attempts to free itself from the impossible situation. He was making money that enabled him to live out here in the desert with its mountains and sage, its blue sky and open lands.

I'm like an animal in a fuckin' trap. I am *an animal in a trap. What did I do that was so bad? I trapped. So this is what they felt like. Maybe it's what I have coming for doing that. Maybe it's because I killed millions of fish. Maybe it's because I killed something else.*

The hydraulic motor continued its high-pitched screak. The deck lights bore down. The 52-foot vessel had become a minute speck on the vast Pacific Ocean.

The 5- by 8-foot steel trawl doors continuously gonged against the steel sides of the boat, reverberated through Larry, but heralded his plight to no one. CLANG. CLANG. CLANG! Unceasing, deafening, they pounded the sides of the boat with the rhythm of the ocean.

As his father's presence eddied beneath the boat, Larry began his solitary version of Odysseus' journey. The melodic Sirens did not sing their songs, but screeched in the hydraulic gears and swooping gulls whose black eyes helled into his soul. Time began to leech his life. *No!* his unconscious cried, *I* will *be Odysseus. I will hang here like Christ tortured beyond life. I will survive to love and watch Lincoln grow, to return to Bev.*

The sheen of the moon danced on the glassy waters of the Pacific.

Chapter 2

Early in Wednesday morning's light David Vandecoevering drove down the hill to the dock. He drove past the history of this once-flourishing Tillamook tribe and its language. He passed by the edge of all memory of the Tillamook huts and fires, all trace of where 150 years earlier men had left before dawn to hunt back up in the woods while women worked quietly and patiently at camps and home to keep the fires, gather wood, dry food, and eye and listen to the children as they played. He approached the area where their wooden canoes had rested between the beach and the forest, where the sand lay warm in spring and summer, where waves, proud and tall, pounded the shore while every member of the tribe worked for days butchering a whale down to its smallest scrap to sustain their subsistence lives, where the men brought in their wooden boats filled with salmon for eating and drying. The women eyed the shore each time to see their family's boat, to watch it cross the crest of the waves and land ashore still upright. No, David did not see the history of the people that preceded him. Neither did he see his parents' house nor Bev and Larry's as he drove past them. All he saw and felt was his own anguish as he continued across Highway 101 and into the dock area where on one side hundreds of trawlers, trollers, and private boats sat silently in their slips, and to the left and ahead canneries and restaurants hummed their business. He could see where the *Fargo* docked. Empty.

He stopped in The Troller, his parents' restaurant, thinking he'd get a cup of coffee.

"Larry's overdue."

His father shot him a glance but said nothing. As lifetime fishermen they both knew all the possibilities that statement contained, none good. He sipped the coffee as they exchanged single syllables but mostly stared. David put his quarter on the counter and his father shoved it back at him with a long look. He took a step back, said his thanks, intended to take the cup but left the quarter and the coffee on the counter.

He headed across the docks to Hoy's and then to Smith's Pacific Shrimp Co. No, they had had no word from Larry since last evening when he called to say the net was coming in and the *Fargo* would head in as soon as they got the load on deck. Within the hour. Twelve hours ago.

A vise clamped the sides of David's head. Visions of the *Fargo*, the weight of its net off portside, fish in the hold shifting, followed by— God forbid—capsize encircled him. He gritted his teeth as he walked to his pickup. He drove home trying not to floor his pickup for the seven-block drive alongside the docks, passed The Troller, across 101, then gunned up the hill.

At 9:30, the phone rang at the local Coast Guard Station.

"Tillamook Bay Coast Guard, Petty Of…"

"David Vandecoevering, skipper of the *Cindy Lou II*, here. The *Fargo*'s overdue. Larry Hills' captaining it and he went out two-manned with Dick Cooley. Dan Fisher cut his hand badly the morning they were going out. Cooley's a greenhorn, new to single-rigged, side-lift trawling. Larry called me last night to say he was bringing on his last load and they were headed in. He called Hoy Bros. to tell them too. Last night about 9:00. He hasn't answered his radio since."

"He may have gone to another port."

"I don't think so. He had fish and he called to say he was coming in."

Fish in the hold. Hauling in a full net. Short-handed. Deck hand on his first trawling trip. Cold weather. A storm blowing in. It didn't sound good. The person on the other end of the phone knew this situation was over his head. He rang into Chief Warrant Officer Robinson's office. Robinson, the commanding officer (CO) at the Tillamook Bay Station in Garibaldi, listened—12 hours overdue, no radio response, deckhand injured and going out with a green hand. Not good. He gave an unusual response.

"You need to call the Coast Guard Station in Astoria. Their number is…"

"I have their number." He hung up.

Robinson told the petty officer who had answered the phone to call Astoria, Newport, and on down the coast.

"The brother-in-law said he already called them, sir."

"You call."

David, following Robinson's suggestion and having an uncomfortable feeling in his gut that something had gone terribly wrong with the *Fargo*, called Station Astoria. Mike Wood, Chief Quartermaster and Operations Center Supervisor on duty at the time, was also the coordinator of Search and Rescue (SAR) missions. He answered the phone.

"The *Fargo*'s overdue…." David finished with the other worrisome details.

Wood heard "two-manned. Should have been three." He assessed the situation as quickly as he wrote the information, including that the third fellow cut his hand.

When you're two-manning a commercial fishing vessel, anything that can go wrong will go wrong. And it'll go wrong twice as fast. Bad season. We have million dollar helos sitting on the ground, personnel trained to fly them, on alert. I gotta make a decision now, 'cause that could be the difference between life and death for those two.

His smile faded to match his now-furrowed brow. Standard operating procedure was to wait 24 hours before upping a case to SAR status, but, unbeknownst to Larry's family for 23 years, Wood, a gentle, soft-spoken person not afraid to take risks, judged better in this case. This young man with a ready smile and blue eyes to match, and, what seemed to be the popular Station Astoria moustache, thought, *No one ever got his ass in trouble for doing too much, and one of our main purposes is to save lives*. He reached over and sounded the SAR alarm. The search for the *Fargo* had now become a group case, thus making the search network broader. Station Astoria also called for harbor searches in Gray's Harbor and Cape Disappointment, Washington, and in Portland and Astoria, Oregon. These turned up nothing.

Needing a SAR plan, Astoria immediately notched the search up another level to a district case, and contacted the 13th District Rescue Coordination Center (RCC, and now called Regional Command Center) in Seattle. Lt. Dave Glenn drove the early morning's black ice to the downtown Federal Building shortly before 6:00 for his 24-hour shift. A slender, mild-mannered man with light brown hair, who always maintained an even keel, was the SAR Mission Coordinator on duty when the call came in not too long after 9:30 that morning.

Meanwhile, when the Tillamook Bay Coast Guard Station had received the call from David Vandecoevering earlier, they knew this rescue was beyond their scope—it would take more than phone calls and their 44-foot cutter to find the *Fargo*. The Tillamook Bay Station determined the *Fargo* was officially missing and they also called Astoria for helicopter support.

In addition, by midmorning, David and his parents, Larry and Lorraine Vandecoevering, the rest of the fleet, and the local Coast Guard had all radioed the *Fargo* multiple times on channel 16 with no results. Channel 16 is the general VHF channel everyone on the coast keeps tuned in. Lorraine drove around Garibaldi while Larry Vandecoevering, between customers coming to the till, called the local cafés and bars that fisherman frequented up and down the Oregon and Washington coasts. All boats, ports and people with VHF radios in their homes knew the *Fargo* was missing, but the calls produced nothing. Larry heard every call, and wept at his inability to make them hear his pleas for rescue.

Chapter 3

Knowing they were on alert and waiting for the SAR plan, Lt. j. g. Ray Shultz and the person who would be his co-pilot, Gary Ellis, also a lieutenant junior grade, waited for the call giving them the location to search. Time has lost who flew the second helicopter that searched on Wednesday. Lt. John Whiddon and Lt. j.g. Mike Moore did a practice flight for Moore's upgrade that day, but did not search until Thursday.

Shultz, a former Marine helicopter pilot for seven years before transferring to the Coast Guard, had far more military and helicopter experience than the usual Coast Guard pilot. Well-respected by his fellow Coast Guardsmen, officers and enlisted described him as by-the-book, hard-charging, serious, and scrupulously honest. Shultz, 5'11" with dark hair and dark eyes, was 34, the same age as the captain of the boat he was about to search for. On one of his earlier rescues, he, as co-pilot for Tom Walters, an exchange pilot from the US Air Force, flew to Mt. St. Helens on May 18, 1980, the day the volcano erupted, to rescue 27 people, 3 dogs, and a boa constrictor.

Shultz's mother had died when one of the farm tractors rolled over on her. He was 13 months old at the time and grew up on the family farm in Indiana learning the meaning of hard work before he was a teenager. His stepmother disked around the fencerows to create a buffer, then turned the tractor over to the 11-year-old boy to finish the job of disking the fields. A work ethic well instilled in him, he got his first paying job when he was 19 and away from the farm. Although quick-witted and occasionally dishing back good repartee, he was not much of a jokester. Unusual for an officer to chum with an enlisted man, Shultz and Wood, the enlisted chief who made the decision to call this case a SAR, often got together when off-duty to cut and split wood, something they both enjoyed. As essential in the military, that casual relationship never took place when they were on duty.

It was close to lunchtime and those in the wardroom got up to get their sandwiches from the fridge. In walked Lt. j.g. Gary Ellis, the man who would be Shultz's co-pilot both Wednesday and Thursday on this SAR. Shultz and any other senior officers there, in preparation for one of the insolent behaviors Ellis wore like his uniform and was known to provide, silently braced themselves as he walked through the wardroom door. Ellis said nothing.

A junior officer, he was hard-charging like Shultz, a constant, reliable person who followed protocol, and was highly regarded by his fellow officers; any pilot was pleased to see him in the cockpit next to him. In the wardroom, however, Ellis could be counted on to throw barbs and crack comments that provided more than a few good laughs. Today was one of those times when someone had anonymously taken a bite from each sandwich in the fridge. It could have been someone else, but most likely, it was Ellis.

"Your wife doesn't feed you breakfast?"

"What?" Ellis replied blandly. "Look, there's a bite out of mine too." It didn't work. They remained convinced it was he.

The practical joking was not limited to the wardroom. Occasionally, Capt. Ciancaglini, the CO at Station Astoria, walked into his office to see an apple placed on his desk, only to go around to the other side to find one bite taken out of it.

What is it that made this group at Astoria so tight? Leadership and these high quality people. Capt. Ciancaglini was one of those leaders who demanded respect, earned it and got it from every officer and enlisted man who served under him. He was tough and fair, took the bitten apple with humor, brooked no error, and demanded quality from everyone. Unique to any good leader, The Ciang, as his people affectionately called him behind his back, insisted pilots debrief their recent SAR cases: what went right and what went wrong, at the AOMs (All Officers Meetings), the purpose being to help their fellow pilots avoid such situations on future flights. Capt. Ciancaglini was a leader not threatened by error, a person who thought it good practice to assist those under him to quickly and wisely correct any potential problem. His goal was to make better pilots to save lives and equipment. Add to this that the winter of 1981-1982 turned out to be the deadliest commercial fishing season in the twentieth century along the Pacific Northwest. Still fresh in everyone's mind the beginning of this February was the loss of Capt. Olson from North Bend and the number of successful and unsuccessful SARs of the season. Under such conditions, Ciancaglini's leadership became key to Station Astoria's high quality and performance.

George MacGillis, also 34, was the flight mechanic on Shultz's helo both days. He has also been the flight mechanic on the aborted flight the previous October to rescue Capt. Olson and his crew. He had grown up in Portland where he spent time as a teenager working at the Portland Yacht Club. After a 7-year stint in the Navy as a diesel mechanic, he transferred to the Coast Guard. Married with a 3-year-old daughter, his wife was pregnant and due within days. However, before the *Fargo* rescue, they knew all was not going well with the pregnancy. The doctors ordered amniocentesis, which revealed underdeveloped fetal lungs. Susan MacGillis needed to remain pregnant longer for the infant to survive. It would be another month before she delivered, and even then their son remained in neonatal ICU for a month.

The on-duty crews busied themselves at their ground assignments while they waited for the SAR plan from the RCC in Seattle.

Chapter 4

Trapped and jolted, Larry's mind turned in strange directions.

Aw, Kinky. My white cat. Aw, my fluffy white cat! That nice, little, warm, white cat. She'll never sit in my lap again. I won't stroke her under the chin, scratch her ears. I should have been nicer to her. I never should have shoved her off my lap. Should have fed her more, given her more treats. Picked her up more. Held her more. I was so mean to her dumping her off my lap when all she wanted was a nice warm place to curl. Warm, white cat. Mea culpa.

"*Fucking solitude!* I want my cat."

I always liked fishing alone as a kid, hiking in the desert between traps or just for the hell of it. Being out there all alone for a day. But this, this is not...this is not....

He tried to suck himself back together and think about the cat and the comfort of solitude whose limits he controlled.

Expecting Larry home that day at the latest, Bev spent Wednesday morning making bread, cookies, and a pot of soup, even though she knew the first thing he would do was unload his fish, clean the boat, then go to bed and sleep for hours, perhaps even a day. She cleaned house and now ready to do her laundry, she left mid-morning carrying the basket across the street to her parents' house. She had plenty of time before Lincoln came home from school; it was only 10:30. She'd have lunch with her mom.

Corky Povenmire, a local fisherman, driving by, stopped and said, "What are you doing?"

"What do you mean, 'what am I doing'? I'm doing my laundry."

"Aren't you worried about Larry?" he asked.

"What are you talking about?" Bev recoiled.

"See you around." Corky shrugged his shoulders but said nothing more as he drove off thinking Larry had turned up and everything was fine, or Bev didn't know yet. Yeah, that was more likely, he thought.

Her laundry scattered in the road as Bev dropped the basket and ran to her parents' house. She immediately feared Larry was the next number on that list of Northwest fishermen who had died at sea.

She took the back steps into her parents' house in two leaps, flung the door open into the length of kitchen and living room, full of silent people with long faces, standing and sitting wherever they found a spot, their faces already anxious and guilty. To a person, they looked up when the door opened, glanced uneasily at Bev, then averted their eyes, sipping their coffee or looking out the window.

"What's going on?" she demanded, while she hung back by the door, reticent to expose herself to the room and people it held. The wood heat in the house had never been so ineffective in warming the chill that ran through each person's heart. Chicken soup, started as soon as Lorraine Vandecoevering had poured her first cup of coffee for the morning, no longer held its promise of a good lunch. The teakettle simmered on the back right burner of the stove and the coffee pot was in constant use.

"Well. The *Fargo*'s missing."

"The rest of the fleet came in last night but not the *Fargo*," someone else offered.

Bev burst into tears. By choice, she did not have a VHF in her house and no one had called her this morning because they did not know how to deal with what they knew would be her intense reaction. Nor did they know how to deal with their own reactions. A fishing community goes about its everyday business unconsciously waiting for the next disaster. It will come and this one landed directly on four Garibaldi families — the Hills, the Cooleys, the Fishers, and the Vandecoeverings. As it turned out, it also landed on one of the Coast Guard families, the MacGillises.

Someone got up from his seat at the table. "I'll try again," but as he approached the VHF on top of the fridge, a voice came over saying, "*Fargo, Fargo, Fargo.* Calling fishing vessel *Fargo.* Come back." Eyes on the electronics, everyone on the water or in the imaginations of those in the Vandecoevering house stretched their vision out to the distant sea, and tasted the silence before Bev gasped and began sobbing.

She did not know some fishermen who had finished short trips and unloaded their catches were having coffee or a well-needed breakfast at The Troller or Miller's Seafood, sharing tales of plugged holds and downs, discussing other aspects of their recent trip and the current weather. They had just put themselves through three to five days of little to no sleep, hard physical labor, and snippets of food when they received word of the missing boat. Dog-tired, some had gone home for a much-needed sleep of the dead. Those at the restaurants called those asleep at home. These men of the Garibaldi fishing fleet just in and exhausted from their labor of the past days, all roused immediately, returned to their vessels, and headed back out to sea to search for Larry, Dick, and the stricken *Fargo.* Independent thinking and living people who may not have two words to share dockside came together without hesitation, without thought for their own safety to look for fellow fishermen in harm's way. This morning they spoke to one another, offered coffee from a thermos and reassuring words of "Yeah, we'll get out there, we'll be out there really soon," as they walked from pickup to boat, started their engines next to one another, backed out, and headed out to sea. Inside their hearts though, as clearly as if written on the walls of the wheelhouse, was that deep foreboding everyone had: *Whatever we find, it's not gonna be good.*

"*Fargo. Fargo. Fargo.* On our way out. Looking for you. *Fargo,*

Fargo, Fargo."

"*Fargo*! *Fargo*! We're out here. What's your position?"

Families and locals kept their vigil in restaurants and homes up and down the coast. They hung on to every word and sound. Even static, any airwave vibration, had people stare at their radios immediately. They hoped, and they waited. On other days, standing by on the radio offers comfort because it lets them know all is well as families on land hear their chatter.

"What's the catch? How much? Where?"

"I got an albatross here picking nets for lunch."

Weather, always the weather, they passed back and forth.

A VHF radio that did not produce wanted information, however, unsettled everyone. All knew the truth of "There but for the grace of God go I."

As the pilots and the crew waited for the specifics of the SAR plan, Lt. Glenn remained keenly aware of the cold weather and, informed the boat was running with a short-handed crew, felt a great sense of urgency as he scrambled into action—the lives of these two men depended on his accurate and quick calculations before the cold air or water caused them to succumb. He plunged into action. Sitting in front of his computer, he entered the *Fargo*'s last known time and location.

With this information and navigational charts at his side, he began the several-hour process to input and run the computer-aided search plan, or CASP in Coast Guard lingo. Glenn had to calculate four factors—surface water motion, ocean current motion, wind, and tides—and their relation to one another. At any point in the world's oceans at any time, the motion of surface waters is the result of resolution of several impetuses. Off the coast of Oregon, first and most fundamental of these is the great Kuroshio current, which sweeps west from Japan and bifurcates against the American coast, sending complex eddies in various directions but fundamentally southward at this latitude. Second, this southward motion then activates the Coriolus effect, which imparts an anticlockwise vector to the moving water. Third, the wind is dragging on the water surface, tending to move it in the same direction the wind is headed. Fourth, the tides, semidiurnal at this latitude, tend to generate currents toward the coast as the tide rises and away from the coast as it falls. Thus, predicting where an object will drift is a complex exercise of resolving these impetuses into a single direction, as much an art as a science.

Based on the numerical data of these four factors Glenn had just entered into the computer, he ran three disaster options: the boat, a life raft, and a man in the water. He had to make the right assessment of the conditions, do the correct calculations, and find the *Fargo*. His results gave him a grid to plot and pass on to pilots for a detailed search. All this in about three hours in order to get helicopters in the air to search before the arrival of winter's early dark. He was scrambling to get the plan done for these two lives depended on his accuracy and speed. Today's computers, EPIRBs (emergency position indicating radio beacon) and GPSs make this a 20-minute process.

Wednesday midmorning the sun shone down on the *Fargo*. The air temperature stayed cold and crisp in the upper 20s. With each passing swell, the steel trawl doors continued to slam against the steel hull of the *Fargo*. The vibrations reverberated throughout the vessel and Larry's body, yet the seas remained calm and no water splashed on deck. Each hour seemed a month, but he had managed to survive the bitter cold night. Alone, and only inches from his dead friend on the world's largest ocean, he tasted the bitterness of his panic and fear. Worse, the singularity of his situation and abject loneliness were gaining. Solitude entered the soles of his feet, then slowly, gradually, inexorably invaded every crevice of skin, bone, and thought. He was beyond weeping as he looked down death's maw with no one to comfort him, knowing he would never see another live person again. He stared into Solitude and

Void as if he had just walked off a page of *Pilgrim's Progress* into the nothingness that is not life. Philosophy be damned. This existentialism was real and there was no exit. He would toss out there until the sea opened its leviathan mouth and swallowed the boat, …and him down to his last synapses.

Science and physiology, though, would not be damned. Caught by the cold and the damp, he continued to chill by the hour. His body temperature had dropped several degrees and he could not stop shivering. He looked for Betelgeuse or any other star to warm him but realized daylight had come.

Somewhere even deeper inside, though, he knew he had to move beyond this cancerous loneliness because it would eat up his guts and hope, and he would die. He couldn't think about that, couldn't think about the absence of his father who hovered on an invisible plane just beneath the surface, yet who buoyed him back into the present. Nor did he focus much on Lincoln, who now hovered above him, around him, inside, outside of him, yet so dangerously close to how he had grown up.

"Damn it!" he screamed louder than he ever had before or ever would again. *"Get out of me! You'll make me die and I'm not gonna go there! I'm gonna fuckin' live till they come and get me!"*

His anger and the gulls, flying and diving toward his face, hair, and eyes brought him back to the immediacy of the moment. He screamed at them, waggled his head back and forth to scare them away. They stayed away for minutes, perched on the gunwale, flying bridge, rigging, or circling the boat, and the cyclic scene began again.

He had already thought every thought possible. Reviewed his life, his marriage. Lived in the desert, seen its artifacts as he hung there. Thought his favorite parts of Shakespeare, watched scenes from King Lear, recited lines from sonnets. All that was irrelevant, though, he craved company. He craved the companionship of Bev. He craved to be free of this torture.

He fought the bight of loneliness by yelling again at the gulls and consciously forcing the blood down his arms. As he looked around for more gulls, he caught sight of his right hand. What an unnatural position it was in. Must have broken that for sure.

Bev had left her laundry unfinished; in fact, someone else gathered it from the middle of the road and carried it into her parents' house, washed, dried, and folded it. But laundry was hardly her concern anymore. She left for Smith's Pacific Shrimp Co. Billy Schreiber should be there and he would be in radio contact with the *Fargo*. Still thinking with a certain element of clarity, she thought Billy could explain to her what had happened, but he was not there and no one knew where he was.

Bev then went to her sister Mary's restaurant, Miller's Seafood and Charters, down by The Troller and Smith's. She could keep a lookout for Billy, listen to the VHF radio at Mary's charter fishing business, and check with people who came in to see if they knew something. The place was redolent with its usual odor—fried food and cigarette smoke. Bev walked to the VHF, picked up the receiver. "*Fargo. Fargo.* Come in *Fargo*. Do you read me, Larry? Over."

Mary looked up at her as she poured her a cup of coffee, hardly what Bev needed, but she sipped it when Mary handed it to her. Bev sat at one of the tables. Fishermen who couldn't go out to search for Larry huddled around the VHF with coffee and cigarettes in hand trying to calm Bev who was on an upward spiral to hysteria.

"Well, Bev, the good news is that no one's found any flotsam," one of the men offered.

That is good news, she quickly thought. At least they haven't sunk. That was soon replaced with the thought what if they had sunk, but no one had found the flotsam yet.

"Do you know where Billy Schreiber is?" She shot the question into the air, hoping it landed on someone. She was now thinking if she could just find Billy, he could locate the *Fargo*. His father owned Smith's Pacific Shrimp Co. and he was in charge in his absence. He would know. He was in charge. He would know. Unable to locate him, Bev believed his wife, Mary, who now embodied Smith's, could locate the boat if no one else could, and finding her became the goal. Finally reached at home, Mary Schreiber came to the docks to take some level of control. She called up and down the coast, yet another person to do so, making sure everyone knew the *Fargo* was missing and that someone would call her as soon as a mayday or SOS call came.

It was getting on lunchtime and Bev's sister, Mary, placed a hamburger in front of her. When she finally took a bite, it tasted like cardboard. Nothing appealed to her but finding Larry.

She walked over to the VHF again. "Come in, *Fargo*. Come in Larry. Do you read me, Larry? Over."

"We got feelers out everywhere, Bev, from Astoria to Coos Bay. Every port up and down the coast knows we're looking for the *Fargo*. If they show up, we'll get a call right away."

"Yah, he's no idiot. He's a good fisherman. Anybody'll go out with him. There's a storm coming in. Only an idiot would stay out on purpose and he ain't no idiot," someone else chimed in.

Someone poked him in the ribs for sounding inconsiderate. "We'll find him, Bev. We'll find him."

Bev's head was spinning and she now heard only parts of conversations. Her sister, Marge, came in, walked up to Bev and folded her into a hug.

"We need to go up to the Coast Guard Station. They'll know something," Bev said to Marge.

"Come on. I'll take you up."

As they left, the fishermen and townspeople glanced at one another, said nothing, and returned to their coffee and cigarettes. They carefully stared away from the table, now avoiding eye contact even with one another.

Chapter 5

Early Wednesday afternoon at about the same time the Garibaldi fishermen were still out looking and two USCG helicopters took off from Astoria, Marge drove Bev up the hill to the small Coast Guard station that overlooked Garibaldi and its harbor. Its main building was classic Coast Guard: a New England white clapboard, two-storey house with the front door in the middle and two windows on either side. The second floor mirrored the first, and both had a porch across the front. The third storey had dormer windows and above that, the captain's walk with a green wrought iron balustrade and a small windowed room inside. The roof was the traditional red tile. Four years earlier Marge had spent many afternoons there after high school because her best friend was the daughter of the officer in charge at the station. She was accustomed to going in through the back door. Even now on official business, she entered through the back door. Someone ushered the two women into a room where Dick Cooley's father and stepmother sat in increasing discomfort. Cooley's father wept continuously. A few years earlier his other son had died. Not knowing about Dick was more than he could bear and he feared the worst. The room was pleasant but sterile, a cold room whose walls had no pictures and whose paint was a neutral color chosen to subdue expression of emotions.

Similar to other fishing communities in the country, Garibaldi's perception was that the Coast Guard's emphasis had changed during this Reagan administration. It seemed their purpose was now to locate drug-carrying boats rather than to perform their traditional search and rescue role. Fishermen up and down both coasts became irritated not getting the usual help they needed, but having their fishing interrupted while the Coast Guard boarded their boats for drug searches. The Reagan administration's Just Say No policy coupled with zero tolerance begat years of what fishermen described as Coast Guard harassment; they boarded fishing boats, sometimes with drawn M-16s, shotguns or 45-caliber pistols. Inexperienced, 19-year-old men right out of boot camp, testosterone pumping through their veins and indoctrination in their heads, wielded this arsenal of weaponry.

Complicating the change in fishermen-Coast Guard relationships was the extension of the Three Mile Limit to the Two Hundred Mile Limit. The long-extant arbitrary territorial border of three miles had been extended to 200 miles off the United States' coasts in an effort to assist the domestic fisheries' small and factory trawlers, and to pursue drug runners. Foreign factory trawlers repeatedly violated this boundary under cover of darkness over-fishing and depleting fish stocks wherever they could, and forcing emergency closures and grounding much of America's trawling fleet. The Coast Guard's hit-and-run tactics protected the fishing grounds as best they could by keeping the huge factory trawlers at bay, but it was a never-ending, understaffed job. These actions also netted the Treasury billions of dollars from illegal drug monies and fines on foreign trawlers caught within the territorial limit. However, with no increase in Coast Guard personnel, people had to come from somewhere within the force; the fishermen perceived they were taken away from search and rescue. The purpose of the Coast Guard since its establishment in 1790 as the Revenue Cutter Service is the protection of national waters. Such protection originated with and still includes incursion by foreign powers and monitoring of illegal activities within the territorial limit. The safety and rescue of boats and people, established in 1848 as the U.S. Life Saving Service, is the second aspect of the Coast Guard's duties.

The two women and the Cooleys sat in the room in the Coast Guard station, full of anxiety and dread, desperately needing their help, yet still on some level aware of the current conflict between their communities and the USCG.

Someone had suggested to Bev and Marge, perhaps when they came in the building, that Larry and Dick might have gone to a bar in another port and were sitting, comfortable and warm, having a couple of beers.

The person coming in to talk to them had given up his outside hope that perhaps they were sitting in another port comfortable and warm. He had ordered the case to group status, but when he called Station Astoria, he learned Vandecoevering's earlier call had done just that.

Were he to learn now they were safe, he'd feel good for the moments before he wondered if he and Wood had made a professional error by acting too soon. Best guesses on a missing vessel, that's what this was about. Entering the room, he felt powerless to respond to the families. He knew it was now a group case, but he knew nothing beyond that. As information moves up, people take it and act on it. There is neither time nor need to pass each small action back down the line; indeed to do that causes confusion and adds stress to the situation. Those on the back of the wave or in the trough behind cannot see and do not realize that. They only know their pain in their wait for the desired resolution. Bev was ready for this Coast Guardsman.

"Just because somebody's not answering their radio doesn't mean they're in crisis."

In her fear of widow's grief, Bev misunderstood what the person said to her. What she heard was that the USCG couldn't start a search for five days or they'd be chasing after every boat missing for a couple of hours.

"Five days!" Bev cried out. "If they're alive and in the water or some other trouble, they'll be dead in less than one day!"

"Listen," Bill Cooley managed to rise out of his dejection long enough to attempt an interjection before Bev cut him off.

"With a full hold, it's damn unlikely Larry would take the *Fargo* anywhere but here! Anyway, before coming up the hill, we already put out feelers in all the bars up and down the coast: 'Is the *Fargo* there? Have you seen Larry or Dick?' And that reliable grapevine, evidently a lot more reliable than you are, has already come back that *no one* has seen Larry or Dick or the *Fargo*." Bev paused for this information to sink in to what she perceived was his thick skull.

What no one in the room knew was that two helicopters were already in the air searching. The Coast Guardsman remained calm. He had no good information to pass on. "Ma'am, we *are* doing everything we can. It may be a day or two before we know more."

Again, Bev misinterpreted him thinking he'd said it would now be two days before they started their search. She careened out of control again. "Even the local fisherman know they're not sitting in a bar somewhere because one minute they saw them and spoke to them and the next minute, gone. They found no lights and got no answer on the radio! Larry is a responsible, seasoned fisherman and we would have heard from him long ago if something weren't wrong. Even the local fishermen are out looking for them right now.

"They were on their way in!" she continued. "Larry called Hoy's yesterday evening and said he was on his last haul back and would be heading in to Garibaldi soon. He'd put the load on deck and head in. That was almost 24 hours ago! Do you really think, with fish in the hold and a deck load, after calling in to the cannery and saying they were heading in to Garibaldi, that my husband is in a bar drinking it up with his buddies while fish rot in his hold and this whole fleet here is out looking for them? The *Fargo* is missing and those men are in trouble. This whole town knows it, the whole coast knows it, our friends are all out looking for them and you sit here in your sterile white room waiting for days to pass before you build a fire under your asses. Do something!" she shouted.

Bev was near hysterics, her voice shaking as she spoke.

"Larry told David he was on his way in. He told Fred that. You think he's going to lie to them? My husband doesn't lie! With a storm coming up, all boats are headed in. Only an idiot would stay out or head to a farther port with 50-knot winds and 20-foot seas coming up! My husband is a good skipper!"

What the Coast Guardsman saw was a hysterical wife and a grief-stricken father. What Bev and Bill knew was that something had gone awfully wrong and that the Coast Guard apparently wasn't listening.

Bill Cooley sat in the room of the station on the hill weeping inconsolably. He knew in his sad and now empty heart that Dick was dead. His tears and sobs became intolerable for Bev. They forced her to look at her own grief and fear, and for an instant, she saw Larry bloated and blue, resting and gently bouncing with the currents along the ocean floor, his eyes open.

She shuddered and shook her head several times as if that would rid her of the horrific image. "Let's get out of here," she whispered to her sister, "I can't hack this. I can't sit here and listen to this crap and watch Bill and still keep my hopes up."

As Bev and Marge walked out the door, Bev, her mind tired and racing, was mumbling her hopes and horrors. She stood in the parking lot of the Coast Guard Station staring inwardly to agony, wondering what to do next, staring outwardly at the Coast Guard building and its perfectly manicured bright green grass beneath the American flag flapping against the intense blue sky and enormous, puffy, white clouds. Her eyes burned in the brilliance after hours of crying.

As if to the sea and her husband it held she whispered, "Why are these things so crystal clear and perfect when life is looking darker and grimmer, and more uncertain? Please, God, let them be all right."

Panic took hold of her again and she remained fixed to the pavement. *It cannot be. It cannot be. It...* and she burst into tears again. Marge opened the car door for her.

Their mother, Lorraine, had just left her house to drive around Garibaldi and the dock; she felt an urgency to do something. Watching her daughter in agony, it was growing harder by the hour for this cheerful and intense woman to maintain any semblance of a positive attitude. Normally active in one of their businesses or some part of community life, Lorraine and Larry Vandecoevering were known to be available 24 hours a day and to keep long hours in their fishing and community work. Lorraine hadn't left the house today except to look for signs of her son-in-law, but she also came away empty-handed and empty-hearted. By midafternoon, the Coast Guard was calling the house periodically to update them—the search continued, but they had made no contact with the *Fargo* or its crew.

Not far away at the east edge of town, the school nestled against the forest on the first range of coastal hills. Its bell rang and Lincoln was one of the many students out the door. In second grade, his skills were well above those of his classmates. With his brown-framed glasses and some books to read at home—*Oh this one to Dad*, he thought, he dashed out the door like everyone else. He knew his father would be home from fishing today since he didn't come in the day before. The walk home was straight down hill a couple of blocks.

"Mommy? Daddy?" Neither of them was home. That's odd, he thought, and crossed the street to his grandparents' house. Different from his mother, who had walked into a house full of people, he walked into an empty house. His grandpa was down at the restaurant; that he knew. His grandma must be also. He saw coffee cups everywhere and figured there must have been a lot of people stopping by earlier. He looked—many of the cups were still half full. Grandma burst the door open. He watched her tears as they flowed down her cheeks and dripped off her chin.

"Oh, Lincoln!" She threw her arms around the boy and cried, "Your father's missing. Everyone's out looking for him." He felt both suffocated and lonely but made no attempt to escape this tight embrace.

His world changed. The boat had not come in. Going to the dock with Daddy, sitting in the captain's chair pretending he was going out to sea, wrestling on the living room floor, listening to Daddy tell stories about the Indians of Eastern Oregon, reading *Treasure Island* or the encyclopedia to Daddy, and all his other memories from the first seven years of his life disappeared as if the events had never occurred.

Lincoln, nor anyone else in the family, remembers where he spent that night or any other night for the next month when Larry's mother and stepfather came to take him to Lakeview to live with them for six months. The Vandecoevering family knows he stayed with someone in the family, but it quickly became irrelevant with which family or families.

Already a young boy separated from his peers by his intelligence, he buried himself even more in books and thoughts rather than in games and pranks. His father was missing, and he felt his mother was missing too for she was hysterical, and then left for months in Portland. Plunged into greater solitude than he comprehended, he began his life anew. At age 7, he was as trapped in solitude as his father in the lines. A vast emptiness had come and taken away the sweetness of childhood and its memories. He lost his stories to tell anyone unless they started with, 'After Dad was caught in the cables....' For the next month, he watched the adults swirl their lives and oceans of words around his father. No one crawled down to his level to ask, "Lincoln, what are you feeling? How are you? Do you know what happened? Are you doing OK, buddy?" He was 33 when first asked how he felt when he learned his father was missing, and had long since forgotten what he thought or how he felt. He just knew no one had asked. Lincoln, and Bev, continued their lives as trapped against the net as Larry. Only no one knew it.

Chapter 6

By afternoon, Larry was becoming delusional. He entered that slippery state between consciousness and unconsciousness, all the while fighting sleep and unconsciousness.

Suddenly, a short man with a snow-white beard and moustache, white hair and of very small stature, stood beside the net reel, talking with a thick Irish brogue.

Where the hell did this guy come from? thought Larry.

"Eh, laddy. Aye, you're in a hell of a fix." The wee man frowned his concern. "Have you ever done the moan?"

"No, I've *never* done the moan," replied Larry.

"Well, I'll show ye." He gave a noisy demonstration quickly breathing in three times and then exhaled, uttering, *"UUUHHHH!"*

"Like that," he stated. "That'll help you deal with the pain."

Larry breathed in deeply three times and let out a three-second moan.

"That's it, Laddy! You just keep doing that. Aye. Good."

The little man evaporated. Schew! Just like that! Gone.

Larry did the moan for hours and hours and hours.

Wednesday's light dimmed as the second night closed in. The wee Irishman did not return; Larry missed his companionship, but he had served his function. The *Fargo*, still idling west-northwest, was at the full mercy of the sea. The stars and their light vanished gradually as the front moved in. The scream of hydraulics, the slamming of the doors against the hull, and the pain in his arms burrowed deeper into Larry as second by second, hour after hour, his moans rose and fell with the ocean rhythms.

What'll happen if a speck of dust gets into the autopilot? Maybe its points need cleaning again. Damn, what if the thing goes off completely and I head into shore with the current? I'll slam into the rocks. The boat will sink. I'll still be strapped to this net reel and nobody's ever going to find us, the boat, me, Dick. We're gone forever. No notice. No explanation. What'll that do to Bev? To Lincoln? They'll live their lives never knowing what happened. There will be that empty hole of no explanation or reason. Lincoln will grow up like I did. That isn't so bad. No! It's terrible! Yes it is. I don't want them not to know. I don't want to slam into those rocks.

Deep within smoldered his father's death. All his mother and he ever knew was that he had died leading his troops in retreat. Had he been killed instantly like Dick? Did he linger waiting for a medic, thinking, talking about his wife and son? What was his agony? Was he alone when he died? Did he die on the ground where he fell? In a field hospital waiting to be chosen out of a triage? Had Larry allowed himself those thoughts, he would have banished them to maintain his will to live; yet that loss and those unanswered, even unasked, questions were what now gave him his strength.

Those doors are going to beat a hole in the side of this boat. Metal fatigue. Damn thing's going to sink. I'm gonna drown. They'll never find me. Why the hell am I out here? and he bargained not to be on the sea, not to be on the Fargo, this boat he was growing to hate. I shouldn't have gone out two-manned. I never should have left on a Friday. Look at me now. I'm the one who's crucified. Bad move, you fucker. Dick'd still be alive. And the binnacle light. That should have told me everything. I'd have been better, cleaned up, to just head in instead of being tired and greedy. I wasn't greedy. I just wanted to make ends meet, let Dick have a good trip. Dick. I am so sorry, man.

"Damn, damn, damn me."

He slid into depression, just got there when a gull flew toward his face. He should have thanked the gull, but he instead he screamed and swore at him.

At the end of the second day, Larry continued to pull, tense, and relax his arms, hoping he was forcing some circulation through them. The radio blared on again, for the twentieth time or more. This time it was Bev.

"Fargo, Fargo!" Her voice trembled. "Larry, can you hear me? The Coast Guard's finally looking. Where are you? I'm worried sick about you. Pick up, pick up. I love you. Please call. David and Fred are out looking for you. I love you."

"Shut up!" He screamed at the radio. Why is it he could get angrier with Bev than anyone else? Is it because she'll forgive him and still love him? Is it one of those simple truths of marriage? He felt angry and sad because she had dimmed his escape with the Irishman. He did not want the radio blaring at him, reminding him of his entrapment. He just wanted to be found, to be rescued and if not, hallucinating was more pleasant than this torture.

Larry's head was about 6 feet from the jammed hydraulics, which, for 30 hours, emitted its constant, loud, shrill scream as the screech of the motor drilled into his ears. He could see the doors about to slam into the hull if he remained aware enough to look. If he didn't, the slamming still reverberated through his body. So intense was his pain, the air against exposed nerves of his broken teeth was indiscernible. His head lolled back and forth in an effort to rid the noise. He continued to do the moan.

He confronted the agony he felt over Dick's death and his own mortality.

"Aw Dick, aw Dick.

"You're really pretty lucky, you know. You died quickly. It's gonna take me a long time to die.

"But this torture can't go on forever."

Marge drove Bev down to the docks. Finding nothing there, they drove out to the North Jetty, the town's Widow's Walk, to their parents' home, back to the restaurant, back to the Coast Guard station where people still knew nothing, round and round several times, then back to the restaurant as daylight began to dim. Once or twice, it was Mary Schreiber who drove her.

Bev again called the *Fargo* from the restaurant. "Come in *Fargo*. Come in Larry. Do you read me? Larry? Over." The radio answered with silence. Bev's moods still alternated between numbness and hysteria, with the hysteria beginning to take over.

She stopped every passing fisherman to ask what he knew. By now, none could look her in the face at all. Bev and her sister ran into their uncle, a State Police sergeant from nearby Tillamook.

"Please help me find Larry," she begged, still hoping for that miracle that would bring him home into her arms. "Please I want to...I...I want to see him. I want to touch his face. I want to see him one more time. I just want that one wish."

"Don't give up. Don't give up," he comforted.

But Bev had given up. It was coming up on a full day since he should have been home. Early Wednesday before the storm hit, her brother, David, and other fishermen had gone to where they'd been fishing and had last seen the *Fargo*. No one found anything—no boat, no flotsam, still no voice or visual contact. By dusk, Bev was out of control, her sentences unfinished and often coming in unrelated sequences. Marge took Bev to their sister Mary's home. Mary called the pharmacy to get a sleeping pill. In Bev's grief and delirium, she now knew people came and went but with little awareness of who or how often.

Chapter 7

The Coast Guard's Station Astoria and 13th District RCC now knew the *Fargo* was neither in its last known location nor in that immediate, general area. This meant it could be anywhere the science and art of Glenn's calculations and best guesses had determined. To search this larger area, the helicopters would use a parallel sweep search. By early afternoon, two HH-3 helicopters took off from Astoria.

One helicopter flew for 4.1 hours in a rectangular, parallel pattern. Beginning at a point determined by Glenn in the CASP, Shultz flew a straight line in one direction as he looked out his forward and side windows and Ellis looked out his. The enlisted men in the rear looked out their respective smaller, single windows. The given search leg of five nautical miles covered, Shultz banked right for one nautical mile then right again. He flew five more miles on the second search leg, banked left for one mile, and then left again for the next five. Continuing this, he thus followed the parallel sweep search plan of the area Glenn had determined the most likely. This rectangular search pattern allowed a half-mile visibility left and right. Each person looked intently for the *Fargo*, a life raft, or two men in the water, hopefully but not necessarily, in orange survival suits. Turn after turn, mile after nautical mile they searched. For three hours Shultz and Ellis searched but sighted nothing. The second helicopter did the same parallel search pattern for an adjacent area but also found nothing. Shultz logged the flight codes for both a

SAR and a training mission. Time has lost who flew the other HH-3 and what its flight duration was. The two helicopters sighted nothing — no boat, no flotsam, no life raft, and no people in the water. Whiddon and Moore also flew that afternoon but on a training upgrade for Moore and not on a SAR.

It was still sunny but the ocean was now growing choppy with the incoming storm. In anticipation of a hoped-for rescue, Shultz flew into the Tillamook Bay area to do a practice hoist training mission in calmer waters. On board was a second flight mechanic, William Clayton. MacGillis, the flight mechanic, operated the winch to lower Clayton, in a mustang suit, from the helicopter.

Low on fuel, at dark, both helicopters returned to Astoria. In Seattle, Glenn spent the night waiting, catnapping, answering other calls, and reviewing his calculations and estimations. With the information the helo crews had not found any sign of the *Fargo* and his review of all information, he determined a wider search area was needed. This meant ratcheting the search up to the fourth and highest level. He contacted the PAC, Pacific Area Command, in Sacramento for C-130 support.

On the front of any storm, winds and ocean currents begin to change before the clouds move in. Quietly at first. The beginning of the change is imperceptible except to a solitary person or fisherman. Not only did Larry know the storm was predicted, he could have narrated its progression while sitting in his living room. Even in his condition, he knew the moment the front began to reach the *Fargo*. He felt the change in the air temperature and the rhythm of the ocean, felt the barest breeze against his skin, knew the whisper of the wind in the rigging was about to come. The undercurrent of his fear rose. His world had reduced to the reel and the back few feet of the boat, and there was a bad storm coming in. It was now the gulls that had the big view — a vast ocean, a small boat, and the delectable face, eyes, and hair — of a living creature who didn't swat them away.

He recoiled from another diving gull and winced as he felt the noticeable roll of the boat. The breeze grew to a small wind. The rain started lightly. Not knowing how bad it would get, he could have cried, but he was so dehydrated and exhausted he had no capacity for tears.

He figured the waves had increased first to 6 feet, then 10, and finally to 15 feet. Whitecaps everywhere doused him, drenched him. He remained pinned to the reel like Odysseus on the mast, his consciousness floating in, above, around him. The Sirens screeched at him as pain and storm tormented him. Gulls pecked him awake. Time leached away his life. But his unconscious kept screaming at him, *I will be Odysseus, I will survive, I will hang here splayed like Christ tortured beyond life. I will survive—love and watch Lincoln grow, return to my Bev.*

Darkness had come. The Coast Guard waited for daylight. The families waited for word from Larry and Dick. Larry waited rescue.

Oh, Larry. Oh Larry! his wife ached for him as the sleeping pill took effect and she drifted off in the early evening. His name tingled through every part of her. He was in her fingertips, her tears. The smell of him was in her clothes, in his jacket she had worn all day and now used for a pillow. She inhaled him with every breath. He was in his son's eyes. Married 10 years, they were still wildly in love. They hadn't reached a point to wonder, even for a moment, what they were doing in this marriage. They remained as adoring as the first time they met, as committed as the day they married, and, onshore in her sister's house, Bev was falling apart at the thought of losing him. Wretchedly for each, their hopes diminished at about the same time that Wednesday night.

The radio blared on intermittently.

"*Fargo. Fargo.* This is the *Willapa Maid.* Come in."

"*FV Fargo.* US Coast Guard calling. Come in please. Come in. *FV Fargo.*"

Incessantly. Irritatingly. In his powerlessness, Larry found himself getting angry at the radio and its varied voices that blended into one and always seemed to turn into Bev's.

As the families of the Oregon coast sat down to supper shortly after dark, events out at sea changed. The foul weather had picked up and a moonless, cloud-cover black crept across the *Fargo* deck and net reel. It covered Larry's body, wove inside his thoughts, and wrapped around Dick. The net reel had become a rack of medieval torture. Hung up to die in an unnatural light, the hydraulics bore an unnatural noise through Larry's nerves, bones, and soul. The night that lay as black as the depth of the ocean floor became interminable.

The boat rolled in the rising swells; the force of the storm was closing in. The *Fargo*'s constant movement increased the stress and pain on Larry's body.

Early in this second night, the big Caterpillar engine had sucked the starboard tank dry. The three fuel tanks of the *Fargo* were connected to the engine by manual valve controls; there was no automatic system to switch to another tank. The instant cessation of noise was abrupt. No engine drone, no hydraulics motor. Stunning silence. Because of his extreme pain, hypothermia, partial loss of reality, and the changing state of events on the boat, Larry did not notice the silence immediately. The net began slipping back a foot or two at a time pulled by the tonnage of the full net dragging in the water just feet below the surface. Ever so slowly the net reel backed a bit more unwrapping its human catch, until it finally jammed again. One sock on, one sock off, Larry was now more upright. The toes and balls of his feet touched the steel deck for the first time in 24 hours. He supported himself somewhat on his legs to relieve the weight of his 200-pound, 6'4" frame from his arms alone. Without cognizance of the events other than his feet on the deck, Larry had shifted positions. Peculiar as it sounds, the partial unwinding of the reel had also changed the tangle of the hose lines and his position. He no longer hung upside down. Not only did his feet now touch the deck, inexplicably his left arm had been pulled under his torso to a position parallel to his right arm. The change was not enough to release him, but just enough to help his feet support him. He now faced not the net reel but the port side of the boat.

The motion of the boat increased. Across the next hour, Larry gradually realized the engine was silent. It would be erroneous, however, to say he had any reprieve. The lack of force from the engines driving the boat, made the boat less stable. The pitching and rocking increased. His feet rested on the cold deck. He could now hear every idle noise — a cup or thermos not put away before the accident, anything not tightly fastened in the engine, engine room or lazarette, dishes in the cupboards. A pot on the stove jackknifed over the 2-inch rim to the galley floor, a cup on the counter rolled back and forth till it also fell over the rim and then broke on the floor.

I can actually get my feet on the deck! I can...Dick...I can see your face. It's kind of frozen. Very...very lifeless. White. Pale. You have no texture, translucent parchment. And spooky. Real spooky. I...I've always hated dead people...and I get stuck face to face with a...dead guy. Just hours ago...you were a friend of mine. I'm not gonna start screaming or anything, but I don't want anybody else to have to look at you like this.

He couldn't stop looking because he was afraid to close his eyes, afraid he'd fall asleep and die. Look like Dick. For the 30 or so minutes it took for the rigging lights to dim then extinguish as the batteries ran down, Larry stared into Dick's pale face, its skin the color and translucency of parchment. But it was not Dick's face; that was under wraps of net. In the ever-paling deck lights of black night, Larry stared straight into his hallucination and the personification of his fear.

Words, stuck in his mind, kept repeating themselves. *Grim. Very...*

very grim. Very grim. The Grim Reaper. Shheww. Very grim. Just...about as grim as it can get.... Horrible. Horrid. Horrid.

He was disoriented enough that it was only after the rigging lights went out he fully realized the small tank had run out of diesel. He hung there, waiting for daylight, waiting to die, waiting in that diminished hope someone would find him, a mote floating on the dark, shrouded, vast ocean of the world. His mental balance continued to deteriorate as his body temperature decreased and his delirium increased. However, he still exercised his arms in the mantra of isometric tightening and loosening. Tightening and loosening. Tightening and loosening. Tightening and loosening.

When the engine stopped, the boat slowed to move in the current. With no one to correct the boat's steering, the weight of the net pulled the stern of the boat portside until the propeller caught it underwater, thus fouling the net. The *Fargo* began to pigtail westward in a course of concentric circles.

When not at the surface, his panic remained an undercurrent. He knew he'd tried for a full day to think of any way out of this snare. Now he realized his situation was even more desperate: It made no sense to try again to pull off his arm. If he kicked the valve, the net wouldn't back out and the diesel stove had gone cold. Escape from the lines had become futile: He had no heat to cauterize blood vessels, no radio to give his position. He was too cold and his hands and arms too damaged to do the necessary steps to switch to the second tank and start the engine again.

The rain increased to wind-driven.

In the middle of the night, a group of cinnamon-colored brown bears appeared on deck. Ice hung off their faces and hair. They padded around the deck, the hump between their shoulders moving as they walked. Larry looked at their big heads and bodies, noticed they had some human facial characteristics—flatter, less extended noses, yet still, their shape, size, and fur told him he had bears for companions.

They spoke a language Larry did not understand, waved and motioned at him to come with them. Oh how he wanted to! While several bears remained in the background, two walked up to him, moved about on deck. He tried to talk to them. Not knowing what language they were speaking, he decided to teach them English. He wanted them to understand the concept he was trying to get across: How to build a fire.

He had lost his hat, boots, and a sock. His clothes under his raingear were wet. He knew he was dangerously cold and would get colder. He had stopped shivering, meaning that his body temperature was now below 91 degrees. His muscles grew rigid and as more and more cells became damaged, his situation became evermore dire. His kidneys were now in danger of severe damage.

If I can just teach these damn bears English, I can teach them to build a fire and I'd get warm again.

His attempts to teach them English failed…they just shuffled around. Larry perceived they were stupid since he couldn't get them to understand what he wanted. Finally, they shuffled off and went away.

The bears returned often that night, in Larry's efforts to warm himself. He was frustrated with them for he knew if he could just get through to them, they'd be able to make the fire and he could get warm again. Much more complicated a task than he realized in his severely hypothermic state, it meant once he had taught the bears English, he'd need to teach them to switch the fuel tank lines and start the engine.

He knew he was pivoting on the edge of life, but he also knew that the leprechaun, bears, and Bev were all there.

Bev stood on the deck, but Larry found her no more cooperative than the bears. She refused to secure down the doors.

BLANG!

He bellowed at her, "Secure those goddamned doors!"

BLANG!

"Bev, secure those fuckin' goddamned doors!"

BLANG!

"BEV, SECURE THOSE GODDAMNED DOORS!"

The storm was full on. The waves continued at 15 feet. They slammed into the boat, unceasingly. The doors battered and clanged against the sides, unceasingly. Added to that, the wind now blew so hard, its incessant, haunting whine shrieked through the rigging.

"Damn wind," he growled then snarled, trying to stop it from beating him up, from sucking the life out of him.

I clamp my teeth together to endure this intense, unrelenting, constant, never-ending, excruciating, fucking pain. At least I have thick hair and a beard. My feet ache. Am I moving my toes or imagining it? One foot off that cold deck, then down and now the other one. Hey, this water is warm. Am I in real trouble or imagining? Are my feet colder than 47 degrees? This pain swims back and forth from my arms to my toes. And everywhere in between.

A blessing and a curse, the jabs, twitches, and spasms of pain kept him from sleep, unconsciousness, and death. His body temperature was now below 90 degrees, on its way down to an eventual and dangerous 85 degrees.

I'm falling deeper and deeper into that cavern of cold. I have shivered, shivered and shivered until I can't shiver anymore. Somewhere I read when you go below 91, you stop shivering. I'm gonna freeze to death. I'm gonna fuckin' freeze to death.

His heartbeat and breathing had slowed dramatically. His lack of oxygen, his pain, and dehydration put him in a stupor, but he continued to breathe as deeply as he could, do the moan, and exercise his constricted arms. He fought and swore for his life, not knowing his kidneys were slowly and inexorably shutting down. Larry was dying.

The cold. The cold. I wasn't meant to die like this. I wasn't meant to die like this.

The stress was more than exhausting. It too was killing him physically, beating him down mentally and emotionally. At great psychological price, he did himself one favor. His neck was exhausted from attempting to keep his head upright while in a forward inclined position. Dick's legs, partially sticking out of the net, were right beside Larry and he had no other alternative. With a piercing emotion and wrenching in his gut, he rested his head against Dick's legs.

At the time of the accident, the *Fargo* was about 20 miles northwest of Neahkahnie Mountain. By now, she had drifted to a position 23 miles off the coast slightly southwest of the Garibaldi Bar, the entrance to Tillamook Bay. She sat dead in water of 240 fathoms at the edge of the continental shelf.

Chapter 8

As the rain pelted him, he tipped his head back trying to assuage his thirst by catching the drops.

In a soft, chanting, and poetic voice, he spoke to Dick, "I am so cold, so scared. And I, and I…if I cross that boundary, …decent place. If I just relax and be dead like you, it'll be so much better. You're the lucky one. I can do this. Go. Quit the fight. Quit the struggle. If I stay over here, I'll stay tortured. If I go where you are…. But my last thoughts… those fuckin' gulls. I'm not religious. I'm not asking God for favors. My energy…schew! It's a better place there than here. Such a struggle to stay alive. Death is good. Why do I fight? I want it. I don't. Step over that line and find out.

"No. I have to fight. I have to fight! Stay cold. Stay!"

"Bev…Lincoln," he stammered between his purple and blistered lips. "Linc, I'll play ball with you. I'll take you fishing when I get better. I'll be a good father. The best."

The last lines of Johnny Cash's *The Highwayman*, began to reverberate through his mind. *I may simply be a single drop of rain/ But I will remain/ And I'll be back again, and again and again and again and again….*

"Coming back, back, back. I'm a raindrop. In a storm. What if they don't find me?"

Larry's eyes closed, his thoughts slowed as he began to slip into unconsciousness.

Sleep. Can't sleep...'cause if I sleep, I'll be colder. Freeze to death. Don't go there! Don't go there!

Parched, his tongue dry, his mouth dropped open with a sucking action that brought him around. He craved water. Crush injuries suck all available water in an attempt to preserve cell structure. He felt no hunger, but in the middle of the largest ocean on the planet, his own body and mouth screamed for hydration. His lips and tongue were covered with large blisters growing black from exposure.

Why am I being punished? What did I do that was so bad? Why am I being strung up like this? I trapped when I was younger. This is what I have coming for doing that. Maybe it's because I killed millions of fish. Maybe it's because I killed something else.

Not the only time he thought this, right out of hell, his eternal punishment continued. Incredibly, the intensity of his torture was about to increase—"You turn that peg just a little tighter and it goes higher."

In any kind of weather, the *Fargo*'s high flying bridge and house forward caught the wind, causing the boat to drift her stern quarter to incoming seas. This meant that now, during the worst of the storm, her windward quarter was directly behind the net reel. The 15-foot waves hit the stern, shot straight up and came back down *right* on him. Some slammed into his face. Others dumped on his head and, in spite of hunching his shoulders, the cold ocean water ran down his back beneath his rain gear. He could tell when the waves were going to slam, and it became part of the water torture. He could hear each wave—coming, cresting, breaking. *Sssssssssssmack!* It hit the stern, exploded to a new crest, and BOOM! dumped on his head or back full force. This went on for hour after hour after hour. Every 15 to 20 seconds. BAM! Sssssssssssmack! BAM! *Sssssssssssmack!* BAM! When the boat was in the trough, waves angled up at about 45 or 50 degrees. The walls of water were the height of the *Fargo*'s flying bridge. In the night, he couldn't see the waves, but he heard them, and he knew their size from his years at sea.

Water splashed over the gunwales as well. His feet, already so cold they were blackened by frostbite, grew wetter and colder as water sloshed the deck. He continued to pick them up one, then the other. The water still felt warm against his feet, even the one without the sock. He felt the rain and with all the strength he could muster, he again painfully and slowly tipped his head back. Mouth wide open, he continued to search for drops to sate his night of thirst. He let his head down on Dick's legs with a collapse that, each time, relieved the stress on his neck.

In addition to this drenching, with each roll of the boat, as one door heaved away from the gunwale, the other slammed in. Side to side, bang to bang, not only did Larry endure the pitch and roll of the boat's motion, the banging of the doors had increased in frequency and intensity. Their vibrations funneled through him like electricity with each thunderous crash. *Boom. Boom. Boom!* Oh, the shots and jolts of pain through his arms, chest, and legs.

He heard the wave hissing at the stern, then *sssssssssssmack!* The starboard door boomed against the gunwale and another wave crashed then smacked down onto Larry. The port door boomed. The wind roared. He heard the next wave with its approaching hiss.

All night long.

It was not the hallucinations that put him over the edge; they were decreasing in spite of his pain and deteriorating physical condition. It was the continuous immersion in waves during the second night and next morning that about drove him crazy: He felt the waves beating him to death with their continuous, intermittent sousing of his head and back as he remained lashed against the reel.

The first rim of dawn lightened the eastern sky above the edge of the mountains. Dehydrated, hypothermic, delirious, and still closer to death, Larry did not see it. He sensed only darkness, thirst, pain, and waves crashing down on him.

The bears returned, shuffled across the deck, in front of, behind him. Again, he tried to teach them English. One bear turned a full circle.

Larry rasped, "Turn!"

As the bear walked toward the house, Larry called out, "Stove! Turn on the stove!"

The bears faded, disappeared.

The doors careened against the side of the boat as it pitched and yawed in the seas. Each slam shattered through him. His thoughts churned.

"Bev!" He called in a croaking yell to her. "Secure those doors! What are you thinking? They'll knock a hole in the sides. We'll sink. Secure the fuckin' doors!" He told her what to do and she wasn't doing a damn thing.

In spite of storm winds whistling through the rigging, the cresting 10- to 15-foot waves, the doors slamming against the gunwales, a pot that kept rolling across the galley floor, and metal against metal coming from the lazarette, Thursday morning Larry felt his world was still. Dead in the water, the *Fargo* had pitched, rolled, swayed, heaved, surged, and yawed with the motion of the seas. Rain pelted him while he continued to move his head still trying to catch as many drops as he could to assuage his intense thirst.

The morning brought one change: When he looked port or starboard, he could see the size of the seas. Because of the height of the net reel, he still could not, however, see the cresting waves as they were about to crash over the stern and down onto him. He continued to hunch his shoulders in an effort to keep the ocean water from going inside his Helly Hansen rain jacket, Hickory cotton shirt, and his wool Duofold long johns, yet all were soaked.

The gulls knew as sure as Pavlov's dogs or Skinner's pigeons when food would come, only instead of meat powder or pellets, it was Larry's hair and eyes they were after. They swooped down again. One hovered above Larry's head, then grabbed a few strands of his hair, tugged them out. Wings outstretched in a blurred flutter, Larry hallucinated a gull swooping toward Dick with intent to peck out his eyes, but it was Larry's eyes that were in danger. He jerked his head to get it away, but not before the gull had once again jerked Larry from his hallucination.

"Augghhh! You goddamned fuckers! Augghhh! *Get the hell away!*" growled Larry and the gull flew off.

More gulls circled the vessel, emitted their high-pitched screech, and careened on air currents, planning the dive. To them, Larry was just other fish in the net. They wanted those eyeballs, easy and nutritious pickings, and anything else they could get off him or Dick's legs and feet. Plain and simple, the men were now merely a part of their food chain. They dove a freefall. Larry saw again and again the swoop and flutter of wings off to his left as five gulls headed their round, bead-black eyes and open, sharp beaks toward Dick's feet. Devils they were, those black-eyed gulls. He whipped his head from side to side, lost in his effort to drive them away.

Only the waves and the gulls kept Larry from lapsing into unconsciousness and death.

FV Fargo at the Garibaldi Docks. (Lowell Schreiber)

David Vandecoevering (center) at the Garibaldi docks in the early 1980s when he was captain of FV Cindy Lou II. Two of his deckhands, Mike Voght and John Ford stand on either side of him. (Tony Vandecoevering)

Larry standing in fish on the Gary Lee out of Eureka, CA in 1976. Notice the trawl net and one of the doors fastened at the side of the boat. (Kenny Kottre)

Dick Cooley's Neahkahnie (Oregon) High School graduation picture. 1971.
(Dorian Studios)

Larry and Bev at their wedding. (Unknown photographer)

The Garibaldi house Bev, Larry, and Lincoln lived in at the time of the accident.
(Juli Blaser Sager)

USCG Station Tillamook Bay, Garibaldi, Oregon. (Abigail Calkin)

Mike Wood at his workstation at Station Astoria. (U.S. Coast Guard)

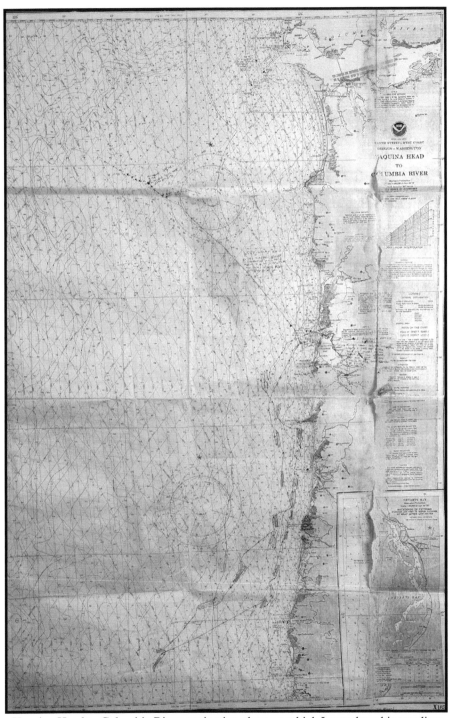

Yaquina Head to Columbia River navigation chart on which Larry drew his trawling route and the back and forth vessel movement. He added the vessel's supposed journey after the accident. (NOAA chart with markings by Larry Hills)

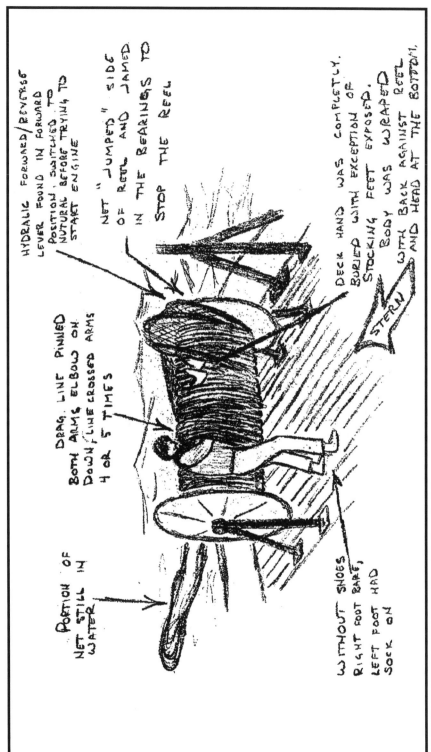

Lutz's drawing of Larry and Dick in the net reel submitted as a part of his official report. (John Lutz)

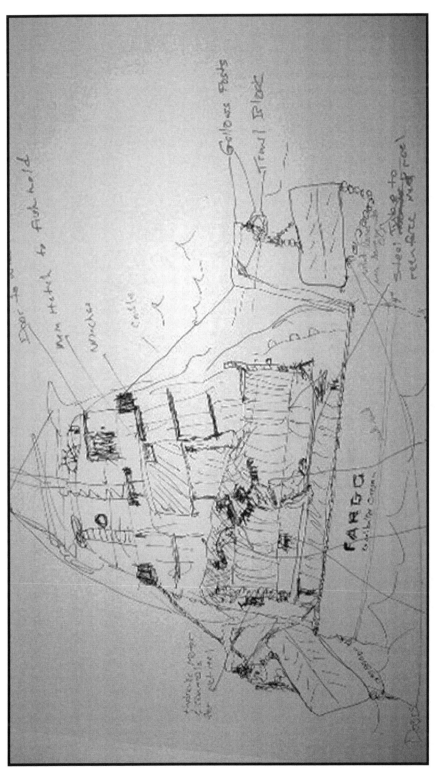

Drawing of the stern view of the Fargo as Larry waited for rescue. This was his position before the fuel tank was on empty. (Larry Hills)

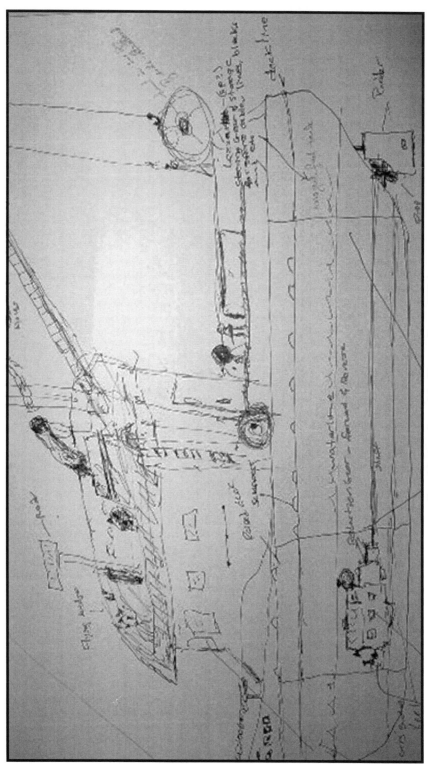

Portside drawing of the Fargo. (Larry Hills)

Appreciation Awards ceremony. Left to right, Capt. Ciancaglini, Lt. jg. Ray Shultz, William Clayton, AT3 John Lutz (shaking hands with Capt. Ciancaglini). (U.S. Coast Guard)

Abigail B. Calkin

John Whiddon the week after the Fargo rescue as he left his helicopter
on a training mission out of Station Astoria. (U.S. Coast Guard)

(L to R) Elizabeth, Susan, and George MacGillis, and
Capt. Ciancaglini. MacGillis was re-enlisting that day. (U.S. Coast Guard)

FV Fargo heading out of Tillamook Bay on a shrimping trip May 3, 1982. It sank later that day. (George Vandecoevering)

L. B. Hills holding his son, Larry. (C. B. Hills)

Lincoln Hills at his birthday picnic at Pittock Park, Portland, Oregon. In early June, Larry is still in the electric wheel-chair, using an extended straw, with his fingers splinted. (Bev Hills)

Lincoln Hills, 2nd grade, at Garibaldi, Oregon Elementary School. (school photographer)

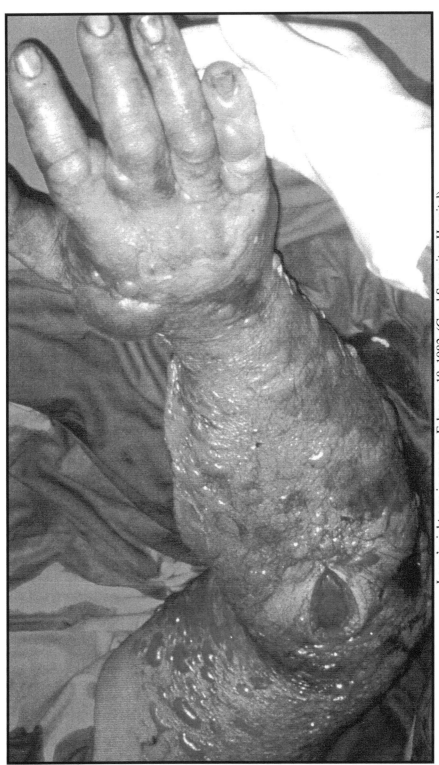

Larry's right arm in surgery, February 18, 1982. (Good Samaritan Hospital)

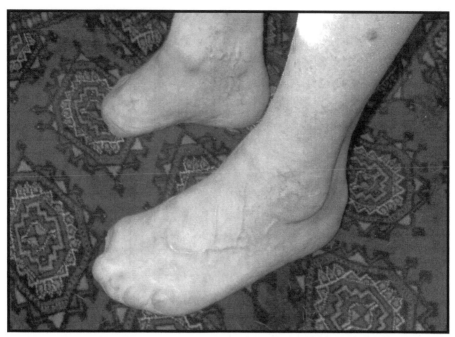

Larry's amputated feet in 2007. (Bev Hills)

Larry Hills placed the nail in the tree with his teeth.
He then used the back of the small axe to pound the nail in. (Abigail Calkin)

The south side of Crane Mountain while hiking the Fremont National Forest Service Trail. (Abigail Calkin)

The Lake County portion of the Fremont National Forest Trail marked with trails and campsites. Larry Hills supervises the maintenance of these trails and has supervised the construction of a majority of them. (U. S. National Forest Service map)

PART IV

SEMPER PARATUS

Semper Paratus (Always Ready)

U.S. Coast Guard motto

Thursday morning a Coast Guard C-130 left the Air Station in Sacramento. The Coast Guard Pacific Area Command, now a part of the search, had sent out one of their C-130s. The C-130, a fixed-wing aircraft large enough to hold a couple of hundred troops in full gear or two Humvees, had become an integral part of military gear during the Vietnam War and was in common use in the Coast Guard. On this occasion, in addition to the two pilots, navigator, radioman, and flight engineer, the plane also had a loadmaster and a drop master positioned behind the cockpit at each of the two large windows in the fuselage. Against the base of these windows was a padded armrest for them to lean on while searching with their binoculars. In the early morning the plane arrived off the coast of Garibaldi to search an area at least five times as large as the area the helicopters had searched the day before and continued to search now. This morning's weather was overcast with broken clouds and rain showers. Visibility varied from a couple of miles to as little as an eighth of a mile. Back and forth on their large rectangular search grids swiping five nautical miles at each pass, the turbo prop looked for the missing boat, its crew, or remnants, knowing the low probability of finding the boat or survivors.

At 12:20 Thursday afternoon, the C-130, CGNR (Coast Guard number) 1502, sighted the boat adrift.

"Got her! Unbelievable," a crewmember declared into his mike as they flew the western edge of the search area. "She's pigtailing to Japan. Right on the edge of our search plan!" It was a lucky break that the Fargo had run out of fuel or the C-130 would not have found her.

"We're going down to have a look," stated the pilot as he careened the aircraft toward the *Fargo* for a lower flyover of the vessel and its occupants.

Pleased they had found the boat, the C-130 again radioed. The RCC in Seattle and Station Astoria picked up the communication, and sent it to the two Pelican helicopters from Astoria—Shultz's 1483 and Whiddon's 1489.

"Vessel at 45 degrees, 30 minutes north, 124 degrees, 13 minutes west." This put the *Fargo* 12 miles west of Tillamook Bay. The C-130 crew estimated the seas at 13 feet and swells at 15. Lt. j.g. Ray Shultz, piloting the HH-3F Pelican, tail number CG 1483, was the closer of the two helicopters and immediately diverted to the area. Lt. John Whiddon, an aircraft commander, piloted the other helo. He had flown Wednesday on a training mission with Lt. j.g. Mike Moore as a part of the pilot's upgrade syllabus that Moore needed to become a flight commander.

Whiddon, with his co-pilot Moore, had searched four hours that morning in the HH-3F Pelican, tail number CG 1489. He had just returned to Astoria to refuel and now picked up a doctor and a Stokes litter. Within minutes the 1489 headed back out.

Larry looked over the top of the reel in the direction of a roar he heard above the wind and ocean. The sound he'd been waiting for, hoping for! He looked up and saw a plane with Coast Guard insignia, just above the water going around, black exhaust from deceleration coming out of the back. He felt an immense surge of relief when he saw the orange and white. He'd been spotted. He would be saved. A smile crossed his face.

I'm not alone anymore! I'm not alone! He's hauling ass going around, not very high off the water, going around me, just going right over the tops of the waves.

"Come on down! Come on down!" Larry was desperate for anyone

to save his life, relieve his pain, and assuage his loneliness.

I know I can hang on. I know I can make it. Someone's spotted me. Somebody's gonna come, thought Larry, then blurted out in his excitement, "Why don't you land right here? *Come on down!*"

The C-130 descended to about 20 to 30 feet above the wave and swell crests. Flying with full flaps at a speed not much over the stall speed of 150 knots, the plane overflew the vessel, then circled back for a second close look.

The pilots and crew saw the feet of a man wrapped in the net and saw the other man spread eagled on the drum, somehow saved from also being wrapped in the net. The one on the drum looked up at the plane, eyes open, head waggling, his mouth opening and closing. They were quite certain the one in the net was dead—how could he possibly be alive?—and the one on the reel was probably alive—he seemed to move in response to their presence.

Lacking confirmation, the co-pilot reported, "We presume one dead. The other appears to be alive." Once again, the Coast Guard had beaten the odds against time.

Even though this was hardly the crew's first rescue mission, that good feeling filled them as they sighted and circled the boat—just doing their job from their point of view—the thrill of one more rescue. The drop master released a marking canister that, on impact, released a cloud of orange smoke.

Jim Miller, Mary's husband, left well before dawn Thursday morning to open their restaurant. Mary stayed home with Bev in case she woke up or there was a call from the Coast Guard. Midmorning David walked in the back door of Mary's home. Neither said hello but they hugged then sat at the kitchen table, each with a cup of coffee. Across the next hour or two, they spoke occasionally and she warmed their cups with more coffee.

"They must ha' rolled over." David spoke as much to himself as

Mary.

"But you didn't find any debris," she countered.

"Maybe they drifted and we were looking in the wrong place."

David stared into the blackness of his coffee. He saw nothing. He felt nothing. Mary stared at the kitchen cupboards but saw only grief.

"I *hate* this waiting!" she announced.

David looked up at her. His square face was drawn, hardened in his efforts to control himself.

He looked out the window. "It stopped raining."

"It's a gray day. It'll start again."

He grunted and took a sip of coffee.

Shortly after 12:30, there was a knock at the front door. David looked up at Mary who sat suddenly horror-stricken. He got up and went to the door. It was Mary Schreiber.

"They found the boat! A Coast Guard C-130 out of Sacramento found the boat. One person's presumed alive. The other presumed dead. Great how they say things, isn't it?"

A knot of hope and dread landed in David's gut. Damn it, he thought. I knew something was terribly wrong.

"Something's still wrong," he turned to his sister Mary. "That's just too weird why there's no communications. Why didn't he send out a.... Why wasn't there any kind of VHF communication? Why wasn't there any flares? Why is he out in this shit?"

His sister glared at his lack of hope. He walked to Mary and Jim's bedroom and shook Bev till she blearily awoke. Mary followed. She washed Bev's face with a dripping wet, cold washcloth several times to wake her.

"They found the boat, and one person's alive, but they don't know who."

Shultz and Whiddon were in the air when they received the call from Astoria stating that the C-130 had sighted the *Fargo*. Both were amazed the turbo prop, anyone, had found the boat. Shultz, the closer of the two, headed toward the scene. Within minutes he saw the plume of orange smoke dissipating, then sighted the *Fargo*. Also on board the helo were his co-pilot—Gary Ellis, and four enlisted men—George MacGillis, John Lutz, William Clayton who was an additional flight mechanic, and a corpsman, the trained medical person, whose name everyone seems to have forgotten. MacGillis was the flight mechanic in charge of the hoist and hoist communication to the pilot and co-pilot up front during a rescue. He was also responsible for the mechanics of the helo including making any necessary emergency in-flight repairs. When asked by phone 23 years later if he was on a 1982 rescue out of Station Astoria, MacGillis replied, "Yah, I remember that. I have PTSD partly because of this. That was the first one and there were a couple other really bad ones." The only Coastie to ask, MacGillis next said, "Did he save his arms?" After that stunning beginning to the phone interview, he also stated it had been a harrowing experience for all involved. It was not the weather, nor was it a dangerous rescue. The danger had already occurred and what they were confronted with was the intensity of the macabre scene on deck.

John Lutz was the avionics man for radio and navigation. He had grown up in Portland, the son of a Lutheran minister. At 23, he had joined the Coast Guard to earn money for college. A bright, young go-getter, he impressed all who came in contact with him with his focus and personality. Like most new recruits, he had pulled galley duty on a ship. This included washing dishes, including officer plates with the Coast Guard insignia while they, the enlisted fellows, ate off plain white plates. Twenty-five years later, on Thanksgiving Day, UPS delivered a parcel containing an officer's plate with the Coast Guard insignia; the return address was Larry's. The plate sits, proudly displayed, on a shelf in the Lutzes living room.

Being one of the sharp ones, Lutz put in for an aviation school to go into avionics—aviation electronics. Twenty-three years old and less than three weeks after completing the required training, receiving his AT3 status and air crew wings, Lutz was on his first rescue involving a death and a near-death. This SAR business was not going to be an easy job.

Shultz approached the *Fargo*, rapidly clicking through tasks and options, his set of skills so well honed that his thoughts and behavior were automatic.

Ellis radioed the *Fargo*. "Coast Guard to *Fargo*. Over."

"Coast Guard to *Fargo*. Over."

Approaching the vessel from the fantail, Shultz flew low and close enough to see the net was partially on the deck, fouled in the hydraulic gear and propeller. Two feet stuck out of the net on the reel. That man had to be dead. The other was trapped in the cable lines but his head was moving. Probably dead. Could be alive. Could be the motion of the boat. His feet barely touched the deck, or as Shultz stated years later in an unaccustomed relaxation of his by-the-book form, "He was on his tippy toes." He saw that he wore no hat but had on wool socks.

Shultz figured the Dead Man Stick wasn't working, but the *Fargo* did not have one. If it had, the moment Dick released his hand from the lever operating the turn of the net reel, the reel would have stopped, thus preventing the severity of the accident. Oregon Commercial Fishing Regulations have never required the presence of a Dead Man Stick on a trawler; as recently as 2010 the boats that have them still do so voluntarily.

There's no textbook solution to this one, crossed Shultz's mind. *We have to put someone on the deck of this boat. Unheard of with all that rigging. Can't be the bow. It's a cleaner place with fewer lines to set someone, but smaller, and I'd be putting him down behind me with no view of the boat. All I'd see would be the ocean. Can't do it if I can't see the boat and what I'm doing. Where's the best spot? Deck in sight. Gotta be somewhere on the stern with the least amount of booms, poles, lines and cables.* He saw one 4-by-4 foot hole among all those lines.

In addition to his own analytic yet fuzzy thoughts about the size of the waves, the empty fuel tank, and getting out of the lines, Larry knew in his head and body that the Coast Guard was present and in charge. Gone was his need to force himself to remain awake and rational. He no longer had to fight to keep himself alive till rescue arrived. He relished the presence of the men in the white and orange aircrafts; they now got to retain all the analyses of the moment. Although it would take him a while to realize it, he was "off duty," could relax a smidgeon, and soon would have someone to talk to.

"Aft starboard corner," Shultz declared.

As Shultz approached the rear of the boat from the bow, Larry turned his head, looked up over his right shoulder at the helicopter. The two men fixed a glance frozen in time. An instantaneous scrutiny of situation and relationship each would remember and spontaneously imitate 23 years later. Larry sat in my living room imitating his own actions as he told me. Shultz described that look by phone. As he turned his head away from the speaker, his voice faded. Unconsciously, Shultz mimed the behavior of the man he had been about to save those many years earlier.

Larry fastened his eyes into the pilot's. Someone staring straight at him. Into his eyes. Into his life. Gonna save him.

Shultz radioed Astoria who patched the message directly to the RCC in Seattle. "We're on the scene. This guy's spread eagle on the drum."

"Oh God!" came the response.

"Yeah. Grisly. We're going to have to lower crew to cut the fellow loose. Avionics and corpsman. They can verify the other fellow's dead."

The RCC officer on duty knew this was a most unusual and critical situation. It was also highly unusual, and risky, to put someone from a helo onto a boat deck, let alone a trawler with all its lines, mast, and booms, with no assist from below. The crew was about to do something they had not done before, but clearly, there was no choice.

"Lutz, get ready to go down," Shultz stated flatly to the avionics man. Although it is now more common, John Lutz was about to be one of the first few USCG members lowered to the deck of a boat during a SAR. This was no training mission. Reality had struck.

"MacGillis. Ready?"

George MacGillis, the flight mechanic, would operate the hoist. He was the communication link between the pilots up front and the crew in the back. He would let the pilots know when, by how much, and in what direction to change position. When he looked out, he spotted a man on the back who looked as if he was doing something, until the helo was low enough they could see better. He saw the cable wrapped over both arms. He shook his head, an involuntary acknowledgment of the crisis below.

As Lutz was getting ready, MacGillis pointed to a back corner of the stern deck and said, "We're aiming for that little corner on the aft starboard side."

Lutz, who decades later would describe the rescue as if it happened last week, nodded as he saw the small square and the crisscross of all those lines between him and that square. He adjusted the horse collar under his arms, clipped himself in, looped his arms across his chest to maintain his position and stability in the collar, then sat down at the door, legs dangling. MacGillis flipped the switch and the hoist picked Lutz up slightly, suspended him, and then began to lower him to the deck of the *Fargo*.

MacGillis continued to operate the hoist, directing Shultz, "Forward and right ten. Man halfway down. Easy left, easy left. Hold...hold," as needed with the 10412 intercom radio line attached to his helmet. As he checked the lines and watched Lutz, he noted whitecaps and 6- to 10-foot waves everywhere. In addition, the rotor wash churned the seas even more around the *Fargo*. This was tricky, lowering Lutz to the deck. MacGillis needed to make sure that John didn't tangle in the boat's rigging, that he knew instantly when to rehoist if an emergency arose. Shultz was doing a great job of maneuvering this helo to make the lowering smooth.

With all his gear on and his arms folded atop the collar, Lutz could not see below him. He no longer saw the specifics of where he was going. Within seconds, he saw the boat's boom swinging, sure it would swat him. Once he was amidst all the rigging, he bent his knees to prepare for the impact of landing on the deck.

MacGillis and Shultz watched as Lutz descended safely. Larry, however, did not notice. All he knew was that the Coast Guard was there to save him and he didn't care how they did it. He relaxed into a semiconscious state, now not caring if he fell asleep, yet also too excited with the presence of people to sleep now.

At 12:32, Lutz's feet hit the starboard corner of the aft deck.

"Man on deck," MacGillis finally declared. He had nailed it! MacGillis had put Lutz onto the only visible and relatively clear area: the one 4- by 4-foot space on this 52-foot trawler. Lutz got out of the collar as fast as he could and flung it away from the boat so the horse collar would not tangle in all the rigging on its way up.

Standing momentarily on the slippery deck of the powerless, pitching and rolling boat, taking deep breaths of air, he radioed the helo on his PRC 90 (personal radio communication), a UHF handheld with half a watt of power, his only communication line. He then walked around to the forward side of the reel by the man spread against the net. Larry's lips and tongue were blackened and swollen from hypothermia and dehydration, his face swollen from exposure, but more, Lutz took in his completely desperate situation.

"I'm John Lutz. I…."

"I knew you'd come. I knew you'd come. I knew you'd come! Thank you. Thank you." Larry was ecstatic to see another person, to talk, to hear a human voice. In these repetitive statements Lutz heard and felt Larry's immense gratitude.

"Take care of my crewman," he requested.

"There's not much I can do for him," Lutz responded.

"Best way...start the engine. Then back me off. Neutral. Switch on the reserve battery bank. Turn the valve to the stern fuel tank. ... The red button."

In this first of many instances across the next 50 minutes as the two men communicated, Larry interrupted one thought with another. He had repeated and repeated over and over to himself his situation and the best way to get out. Now, with someone to listen and get him out, he had hit that moment in time when his thinking raced far faster than anyone can talk. As ideas and images tumbled into thoughts, he uttered them.

"Hey, I'm going to get you out of here." Lutz's voice was compassionate and matter-of-fact. He didn't know boats, but he figured if starting the engine was what Larry told him, then that's what Larry would do if he, John Lutz, were caught on the reel. Larry's mention of putting the engine in neutral made him think about the gears on the reel. Gears he knew, and the one on the reel was in the forward position. Realizing the potential threat to Larry's life if the reel moved, he shifted its gears to neutral.

He radioed up. Ellis, the co-pilot, handled radio communication and kept the flight log. "There's one wrapped in the net and he's dead. The other fellow's alive but critically hypothermic. I can barely understand him, and before he finishes something, he starts on something else. I'm going to try to start the engine."

"OK Lutz," came Ellis' reply.

"He wants water."

After quick communication from the helo to Station Astoria and the RCC came the reply, "No water! A definite no!"

"Yes sir, no water."

Lutz went down into the engine room, shifted the engine to neutral, then ran back up to Larry to check on what to do next as well as to update him on progress.

"Spray ether into the engine. Glow plugs. Then it'll start."

Even concentrating and focusing Larry's words, Lutz had difficulty comprehending his speech, the blisters in his mouth making most of his consonants disappear into rambling mumbles.

After several such trips, all that remained was to switch to the reserve battery, turn the rheostat control knob, and push the starter button. Larry kept giving him the wrong location of the rheostat and Lutz couldn't find it. On his next trip back up, he knew he was wasting valuable time.

"I keep passing the tool locker. Do you have a hacksaw in there?"

"Yeah, and some.... In the wheelhouse. Use it to cut these cables. Package of blades. Friday."

Once again, Lutz hurried across the deck, into the wheelhouse. Opening the tool locker, he grabbed the hacksaw and an extra package of blades. It was now 12:56; he had been on the *Fargo* 24 minutes.

These are rusty and old, he thought, but they'll have to do. Still in their original package, the blades were not old; they were the new ones Larry had bought Friday morning, the day he left on the trip. Over the week, the salt air had rusted them. Dashing back to Larry as quickly as the slippery, wet deck would allow, he grabbed the gunwale, pausing for a few seconds to right himself. Being down in the engine room that smelled of diesel, looking in the toolbox, and not keeping his eye on the horizon, had made him nauseous. He knew why he'd gone into aviation: He had no stomach for boats, literally. Back at the reel, he gripped the hacksaw and concentrated on cutting the cable. He was through the steel-imbedded rubber coating and into the steel cable itself when the first blade became too dull to use. Oh, this was all he needed...to put in a new blade as he stood on this slippery, pitching and rolling deck. He did it quickly, however, then sawed the cable line again. The second blade wore out. He was making no progress. Another blade. This time he made it through! Elated, he started to unwind cable. His good feeling was short-lived: The cable crisscrossed itself into a ball of tangles.

These trips to the engine room and cutting this cable, my adrenaline's running out. Wow, the motion of this boat is making me seasick. Come on, John, he said to himself, *Stay with it. You gotta keep going.*

Lutz still had to concentrate intensely to understand Larry, who was clearly suffering from extreme exhaustion and pain. His jumping from topic to topic and his swollen, blackened tongue didn't make directions easy. In addition, Larry was in that slippery spot between consciousness and unconsciousness.

Shultz and MacGillis looked on as the men in the helo continued to wait in their hover. Lutz had been on the *Fargo* for 40 minutes now. Coast Guard protocol controlled their personal reactions to the horror, allowing them to function as the necessary rescuers in this crisis. Shultz and MacGillis could see things were taking too long and not going well. Ellis, on the radio with Lutz, confirmed this.

"Lutz!" It was Ellis. "How's it coming?"

Lutz hit his radio button. "Not good, sir," he radioed back. "I just wore out three blades and broke two on this line. I got through only one mark of cable, but the rest of it is very twisted. Can't unwrap it without more cutting. The hacksaw isn't going to do it. I can't get him undone. Also can't get the engine started. Batteries are dead. The starter sparks but that's all. I need some assistance. Can't do this without bolt cutters. Any more ideas?"

Shultz radioed Astoria again. This time when Seattle's RCC radioed Station Astoria for additional ideas, Mike Wood clearly remembered his call yesterday from David Vandecoevering, the fisherman everyone in Garibaldi knew was familiar with the *Fargo*. If anyone could, he would be able to start the engine. No one remembers who suggested a local fisherman, but it was probably Wood. Vandecoevering seemed the best and only option. All options were reviewed and the decision was made within five minutes. The idea of an acetylene torch had been bantered about but abandoned. To lower a tank to the pitching boat was far too dangerous—one hit and the boat, and probably the helo, would explode

126

in one fiery ball.

Leaving Astoria after refueling, Whiddon and his 1489 landed at Tillamook Bay's North Jetty to pick up two fishermen.

Ellis radioed back to Lutz.

"We're sending the corpsman down."

"Good to go, sir."

When the Tillamook Bay Coast Guard Station, located in Garibaldi, contacted David, they told him both men were tangled in the winch with one person presumed dead and one presumed alive, and they needed his help on deck. Boats were David's life. He'd grown up around and on them and had worked trawlers, shrimpers and other boats for 12 years. He worked on the *Fargo* as a teenager in 1971, the year Larry and Bev met. Now 26, he had had command of his first fishing boat at 19. He and his father had bought boats in the Gulf of Mexico. David had taken them through the Panama Canal, and up the coast to Garibaldi. He had worked on the *Fargo* and knew it well. He had worked around Larry for seven years and now Larry was captain of the *Fargo* and David captain of a partner boat, the *Cindy Lou II*.

Are they both dead? Both alive? His thoughts flipped around. *Yah, both alive, both alive.* The words repeated in his head. *One presumed dead. Larry alive but Dick dead, Dick alive but Larry dead.* Whether he poured himself a cup of coffee, called his parents, drove to the dock, his movements had become automatic. Only when he looked at Bev or spoke to her did his emotions lunge to the surface and tighten his throat.

"Fred. David here," he announced over the phone. "They found the *Fargo*."

Fred said nothing. Like David, he knew all could not be right on deck.

"One of 'em's alive, one dead. I'm going out. They don't know the boat. I do."

"David..."

"Yah?"

"That's good news, and I'm so sorry." Fred knew how close David was to both men.

"Thanks."

Simultaneously in two parts of town, David and Fred climbed into their pickups, gripped their steering wheels as if they were loose and sped to the helicopter pad on the North Jetty. At the Coast Guard Station in Garibaldi, someone grabbed two bolt cutters and raced to the North Jetty.

David found Fred at the helipad.

"Hey, Fred. What you doing here?" David asked, even though he knew why.

"I just agreed to go out with you. We were both out at the shale pile. I came in right before Larry," he said.

"I should have waited," he blurted. In fact, that was one of his frequent thoughts ever since David had called him to say the *Fargo* was missing and he'd been one of those who'd gone back out in the initial search.

"What do you know?" Fred asked.

"I know that boat. First dragger I ever worked on. They can't start any of that equipment so they want me out there. One's presumed dead. One presumed alive. That's all I got."

Fred looked at him quizzically but said nothing as he watched the helicopter descend, a familiar sight from his air traffic controller days.

At 1:16, the second helicopter, HH-3F Pelican, tail number 1489, with pilot Lt. Whiddon and co-pilot Lt. j.g. Moore, landed at the North Jetty of Tillamook Bay. David stared as the helicopter descended, heard the blades but saw only the *Fargo*. Given the circumstances, the experience of his first helicopter flight was so lost to him, he might as well have been getting back into his pickup. As the two men boarded, a Guardsman handed the bolt cutters to the avionics man who placed them in the Stokes litter. Two minutes later, the helo lifted and turned toward the sea.

Little did Whiddon and David know that their paths would cross 27 years later. Whiddon, now owning a franchise of Pacific Seafood, was at the docks visiting one of their plants in Astoria as David unloaded the catch he was delivering to Pacific Seafood. Whiddon was on the dock taking photographs of the unloading, and the two men talked fish and prices, said their goodbyes. As Whiddon walked away from Vandecoevering's boat, a Coast Guard helo flew overhead. "Brings back memories," he said.

"Oh really?"

"Yes. I was stationed here."

"When?"

"1981 to 1985," said Whiddon.

"Did you ever hear of the *Fargo*?"

"Yes, I flew that one. Lifted the skipper off the vessel," and the new conversation began.

David called his mother, so excited he was yelling into the phone, and handed the phone to John to talk to her. A deeply touching call reported Lorraine. The former pilot realized he had taken David out, but David did not piece together that he and John Whiddon had, in a sense, met before. David became flustered when he realized the connection. After their second goodbyes, the men parted with a hug, which reflected their discovery and filled in one more piece of the puzzle of rescue and relationships. David then called Larry.

On the in-flight frequency, the intercom system within the helo, Shultz radioed for MacGillis to lower the corpsman. MacGillis, with a hot mic (hot mike) in his helmet to leave his hands free to operate the hoist, turned to the corpsman. Ellis radioed Astoria to tell them MacGillis was lowering the second man. Still on line, Ellis blurted,

"Aah! Hold on! Got another problem here."

When MacGillis turned to the corpsman to hand him the harness, his eyebrows lowered in a short, quick frown. The fellow sat rigid, his hands so firmly grasping the seat, his fingers were white. "I can't swim. I can't swim," he kept saying. This fellow refused to go.

MacGillis gawked at him in disbelief, then repeated for him to unfasten his belt and get ready to descend.

"You're not going down to swim. You're going to the deck of the boat."

The corpsman still refused.

"Get out of that seat and into the harness!" Ellis, the co-pilot, ordered him down.

The man didn't move.

Shultz, the senior officer, growing increasingly irritated with his insubordination, sharply ordered him down more than once. The corpsman did not move. Phil Snodgrass, chief petty officer in charge of personnel at Air Station Astoria, noted the USCG had just begun to offer training to corpsmen to go down to unusual situations like these. The rule stood, then as now, a person can decline to go down due to unsafe conditions. No amount of MacGillis' quick orders, talking or coaxing could get this ashen-faced fellow to move. No amount of officers' orders could get him to move. He had panicked and sat paralyzed in his seat.

You can't white-knuckle it now. If this helo goes down, thought MacGillis, *you'll go down with it. You wouldn't even bail out.* He tried once more, "Go! This is an emergency!"

"No," came the stuttered and weak reply.

Furious when he heard that again, Shultz clenched his teeth.

"He's frozen. Useless," MacGillis radioed to Shultz. "I'm going down. I worked with small boats for 20 years and was a diesel mech in the Navy," he declared, unnecessarily reminding Shultz's keen memory of his experience. Clayton, a responsible and competent fellow, could lower MacGillis.

"Do it, MacGillis," replied Shultz.

"Roger, sir."

Transmissions between Shultz in his helo and Chief Petty Officer Wood in the Station Astoria ops center, and then from Wood to Seattle's RCC and back down the line to Shultz, again became rapid-fire.

"The hacksaw blades still keep breaking. What next?"

"How thick is the line he's trying to cut?"

"How thick is the cable?" Shultz asked Lutz.

"About an inch and a half. Steel, an inch, then encased in hose line imbedded with steel fragments, sir."

Shultz repeated Lutz's words to the RCC.

"Any bolt cutters on board?"

"No."

"The 89 just left Garibaldi with two fishermen. They're bringing bolt cutters."

Unhooking himself from the radio, MacGillis put the horse collar over his head and around his chest, clipped it, checked it, and sat at the door. Clayton flipped the switch and MacGillis slid out the door, hoisted first up, hanging in that moment of suspension before Clayton lowered him. MacGillis uttered a quick prayer, "Oh God, help me out on this one." The winds and seas were increasing. Ellis entered in his log:

"1321   45°32N 124°31W LOWERED MACGILLIS

1 PERSON DEFINITELY ALIVE

SEA AND WINDS STARTING TO KICK UP

WINDS 15 KTS. SEAS 6-8 FT."

Descending, MacGillis saw the ocean current swing the stern of the boat away from under him. The next thing he knew he was in the trough between waves and the *Fargo* was above him. Then he was out of the water—on top of a wave—at eye level with the tipped rigging of the rolling boat, looking down at the deck. Next again, he was in a trough with the boat towering above him. A wave crested over him and he was aware he was under water. Clayton raised him, then lowered him to the boat deck. However, once again he was not above the deck but in another trough. More water seeped in his wrist, ankle, and neck cuffs; MacGillis was getting wet, decidedly cold, and beginning to shiver. It wouldn't take too much to make this situation worse. He signaled to go back up but for some reason MacGillis could not figure out, Clayton did not re-hoist him. For the first time, fear gripped him. Right or wrong, committing himself to the water seemed the safer alternative. His heart pounding, he released himself from the horse collar and dropped. He landed no more than 15 feet from the vessel. He grabbed at anything, got fistfuls of water.

For a month MacGillis had known that his wife's pregnancy had serious medical problems that could preclude survival *in utero* or at birth. The doctors wanted to delay the delivery date as long as possible. That's never good news. Now he found himself in the water, knowing he was not a good swimmer and wondering if he'd survive to see his 3-year-old daughter and the unborn child or leave his wife with two deaths to cope with. When Lutz saw him in the water and reached over the gunwale to help him aboard, he saw a look of utter terror on MacGillis' face.

MacGillis knew he had to get out of the water, but he didn't think about his own survival. He just thought about how to get on the boat. As best he and Lutz remembered, Lutz reached over and grabbed him. To avoid the next wave washing him off the fish-slippery deck, he stabilized himself against the gunwale. MacGillis had landed in what he estimated were 15- to 18-foot seas. Larry, still with a surprising level of awareness of the Coast Guard's presence and his surroundings, estimated them as 10 to 12 feet. From the helo, Ellis estimated 6 to 8 feet. Nor would there later be consensus. Shultz stated the boat was pitching, as it would with no power and at the full mercy of the sea, but they were not bad seas. Moore saw the seas relatively calm without significant pitch or spindrift. By the time of the rescue, the weather had calmed from Wednesday night, but it would worsen again across the next hours. Shultz, Whiddon, and Moore, pilots who have been on rescues where the weather and seas were so bad neither boats nor helicopters should have been out, all stated weather was not the factor in this rescue and clearly, they were right.

Shultz remained focused on the scene and the safety of his craft and crew, and on his communication with Astoria regarding the total scene. Whatever happened among the crewmembers of CG 1483, Shultz was right, the specifics that occurred were tough, unique, and did not follow any textbook. In spite of this, the rescue was proceeding. Two people were now on deck with Larry, and from his perspective, they spoke English! His excruciating pain and bone-chilling cold remained ever present, but his soul felt warm for he was not alone. A helo hummed overhead, a C-130 circled at 1,500 feet, and he was in the process of being rescued.

MacGillis assessed Larry as alive but not by much. The other fisherman must have had every bone in his body broken. He radioed Larry's condition to the helo: Alive but in bad shape. Completely out of it and so cold, neither he nor Lutz were sure how or why he was still alive.

During the 18-minute flight from the Garibaldi North Jetty to the *Fargo*, no one spoke about the upcoming scene. Whiddon and co-pilot Moore, their function to fly safely in a rescue, had no better idea than David or Fred what the situation on deck was.

David agonized obsessively about whom, if either, was alive. Was it his good and longtime friend, Dick? Was it his friend and sister's husband, Larry? If it were anything tangible, an arm that hurt, he could have cradled his arm, but now, what pained him, gnawed at him were his thoughts and feelings. He rested his elbow against the frame of the window, head in hand, not even noticing the vibration of the helicopter that rippled through him.

Got to get out there. They didn't tell me who was deceased. Is it my brother? Is it my friend? I mean, is it my brother-in-law? If it's Larry, how am I going to tell Bev? He felt the bottom fall out of Bev's world as if it were his own. *How do I tell Lincoln his daddy died?* He replaced that thought instantly because it ripped his heart out.

If it was Dick, how's Larry going to deal with this? He was flooded with memories of Dick, this fellow he'd known half his life. He'd hired him for a deckhand. Recommended him to his brother-in-law, Dave Jordan, and to Larry as well and Dick had deck-handed for both of them. Dick had gone to school with his older sister, Mary.

He now knew the boat hadn't rolled so he tried to imagine scenes on deck. Impossible.

What happened? How did it happen? How in the hell did they both get in the winch? What freak thing happened? Too odd. Something's very wrong. Why couldn't he have shot out a flare? Why couldn't he have put out a mayday? For the short flight that lasted seconds and forever, his gut churned as one thought after another careened through him.

He recognized the *Fargo* from afar and impatiently watched the distance from the helicopter to the boat diminish. The men in the helo viewed the scene—a disabled boat and the other helo overhead. As they drew closer, the shock of it all came into full focus—two feet sticking out of the net, the other man caught by his arms in the cable lines, and the net fouled in the hydraulic motor and the propeller. At 1:36, the 1489 arrived on the scene and hovered momentarily at 65 to 70 feet above the deck.

Aghast, Whiddon looked below and quickly took in the scene. The man who had died was wrapped around the net reel backward, his body so contorted he had to have broken his back. Worse, thought Whiddon, what a *horrible* experience for the guy who's still alive, eerie that he's so close, just mere inches from the dead fellow. Hanging by his arms, trapped, next to his dead companion for all that time, *What,* Whiddon wondered, *can possibly be the thoughts of the survivor?* Weather was not the issue; the drama was on the deck below him. Amazed anyone survived, after his retirement he would describe it as the most bizarre set of circumstances he'd ever flown to in all his rescues.

A sight etched in David's mind that would never leave: Arms and legs sticking out, bodies—*two* bodies—*entangled* in the net and lines. When he saw both were on the reel and not in the winch as he'd been mistakenly told, he sucked in air. Automatically, he snapped his fingers, and declared unemotionally, "I gotta get down there."

David had never dealt with any tragedy before. Both his parents and all seven siblings were alive and healthy. He'd never come across a fatal car accident or been involved in a fishing disaster. Now here he was, confronted by two people he knew well in a most horrible situation.

Something's.... Is that one of them moving? The rocking of the boat? Those are rough seas down there. It's gotta be the boat. Nah, it's him. Who? Dick? Larry? The man on the top of the reel turned his face toward the hovering helicopter and David caught sight of a partial face looking up—dazed, open-mouthed, numb, mute, neither sensing nor alert. The head dropped down, and it was a glimpse too quick for David to know for sure who it was, but from his split second glance, he suspicioned Larry. *Whoever it is, he knows something's going on. Maybe it's just the boat rocking that gives that movement of his head. Maybe I'm dreaming.... Hoping....*

O God, why can't they both be alive? he implored.

Whiddon confronted different weather conditions from Shultz. The seas had kicked up and the wind now blew 15 to 20 knots. Broken clouds made visibility about five miles. Waves broke against and over the stern and gunwale. In the wake of the rotor wash from the two helos, spray flew through the air in every direction. Whiddon maneuvered his craft to lower the two additional people onto this fully rigged, pitching trawler dead in the water in 10-foot seas. The flight mechanic looked out the door at the mast, seas, deck, and hoist arm in his quick assessment as he prepared to lower David. Due to the increased weather, his calls of forward and right 15....hold forward....easy right...hold, changed more frequently than had those of MacGillis to Shultz. In any helicopter, it

is the flight mech who, at this time, is the person flying the helo. He
has become the eyes of the pilot because the pilot cannot always see the
target he is aiming for. The flight mechanic calls the positions over the
hot mic accordingly. Whiddon positioned and repositioned the helo to
aim for the 4- by 4-foot area in the right aft corner. Shultz had stayed
as long as he could—he knew that he, like all pilots, preferred not to be
out there over the ocean alone with his helo and crew. He had remained
riveted to the scene and its outcome, but low on fuel, he had to turn and
head toward Astoria. The C-130 remained circling at its same altitude.

David was oblivious to any risk he was about to take. Getting on
that deck was far more important. The flight mechanic helped him into
the horse collar and fastened its clip to the winch that would lower him.
The man hollered a few things, but David, his thoughts already on deck,
nodded and yelled back, "Yah, yah," without registering anything said
to him.

It was 1:43, seven minutes from the time Whiddon's 1489 arrived,
when the flight mechanic lowered David down through a small opening
among the rigging and mast toward the *Fargo*. He landed without
incident and hurried toward Larry; he'd been in much worse pitches
and rolls. *It's Larry! Is he alive? Yes! He* is *alive*. The flight mechanic
reeled the hoist line back up. Having forgotten to release himself from
the horse collar, David's feet left the deck and he was ascending into
the rigging. The boat continued to rock in the seas and David suddenly
found himself next to and buffeting against the top of the mast. He
swung like a pendulum on the end of the helicopter hoist as the mast
pitched back and forth with each motion of the waves. He lacked,
however, any sense of fear for himself at this moment.

I gotta get back down on deck. Larry's alive! were his only thoughts.

"Larry's alive!" he almost shouted the words. His joy for Larry,
Bev, and Lincoln overwhelmed him as deeply and immediately as his
emptiness for Dick, his school buddy, deckhand, and his friend. He
felt a mass of emotions so numerous, so strong, so intense, all in such

conflict, he could not separate them. Words did not cross his mind. He could not articulate the emotions of these moments any better than he could have held a drop of water between his thumb and forefinger.

Whiddon and the flight mechanic saw the situation and the flight mech acted immediately relowering Vandecoevering. David quickly got out of the harness. The instant he looked at Dick's legs, he saw he was most certainly crushed. David's quick scan of the deck told him the two Coast Guardsmen were nauseated—sick from the gruesome scene they'd been sent to save, and seasick as well.

But MacGillis wasn't seasick. David's mistaken impression of his behavior came from MacGillis pain and lack of efficient use of his hand, and from possible mild hypothermia after being in the 47-degree Pacific. At some point in attempting to assist David in his landing on the *Fargo*, MacGillis had grabbed the gunwale to stabilize himself. At that moment, the trawl door in one of its frequent slams against the boat, caught his right hand and broke it. He was lucky it had not been crushed and that he was left-handed. However, his broken hand, throbbing when he tried to use it, now hampered his ability to assist.

Thrilled beyond words to see Larry alive, David ran up to him and threw his arms around him, held him in that moment of pure joy.

Larry wondered why a Coast Guardsman was hugging him until he looked down at the deck and saw David's fancy new boots with their brass harness rings, the ones he'd been teasing him about having bought the day before they and several other boats left on this fair weather trip. It wasn't a Coastie, it was his brother-in-law. "Oh! David!" he cried out, now understanding the hug. David held Larry briefly, warmly, then dashed through the wheelhouse and into Larry's stateroom, grabbed his sleeping bag off his bunk, ran back to Larry and threw it around him. With some protection from the wind, Larry began to feel warmth creep gradually through him.

Larry had not realized how hard Lutz had worked, but with the comfort of his brother-in-law present, he thought, *Something's beginning to happen! This shit will soon be over.*

"Water, David. I need water."

David could see his lips were dry, black, cracked, and sun-, wind-, and salt-burned.

"Hey," he shouted. "This guy needs water!" He wanted to dump a gallon down him.

"No water," Lutz declared. "He's got crush injuries. They shut down the kidneys. No water."

David winced.

Every crisis needs one person in charge, and one person only. Usually, it's the first person on the scene. In a sea rescue, the logical person is the Coast Guardsman, but it doesn't matter who it is. On the deck of the boat in this rescue, David knew the boat, trawling, and had been in worse weather and seas. He took charge. Reality kicked in and he plunged into action.

Vandecoevering and Lutz went down to the engine room to attempt to start the vessel while MacGillis grabbed the trail line and awaited Fred's descent. Since the accident had happened at night when the deck lights were on, there was no charge left in the batteries. David switched to the bank of unused batteries, bled the injectors, then tried the motor. As he started the engine, Lutz stood by with a fire extinguisher. Sparks flew from the battery terminals. With a wrench from the tool locker they tried to fix the terminal. No luck. The engine stuttered several times but still would not start. However, there was now enough power to run the VHF radio in the wheelhouse. The two men decided to waste no further time on the engine. No guarantees. Gotta get Larry out first. They gave up and returned to the deck, bolting the engine room door to make it airtight.

David had been on deck for six minutes when Fred Hamann, now in the harness, was lowered to the *Fargo.*

David felt frustrated and muttered as much to himself as to Lutz, "I can't do anything. I can't start the engine. That'd be the worst thing for Larry, because he's already in the reel and that'd mean flopping him back up, reversing the procedure. That would just worsen his situation. But he's alive and I'm just so happy to see that." He did not realize Lutz had put the drum's hydraulic motor into neutral as one of his first actions on the vessel.

David noticed Larry was blacking out occasionally and moved quickly, acting on his own urgent need to get him to a hospital as soon as possible.

The two fishermen went to the net reel while the 1489 lowered the Stokes litter. MacGillis and Lutz guided it the last 6 feet to the deck. At 1:58, the flight mechanic lowered the Stokes litter with the two bolt cutters nested and fastened in it. Lutz unhooked the litter and threw the hoist line clear of the boat.

David grabbed both bolt cutters, handed one to Fred and the two of them started cutting the cable into sections. At first, they had no better luck with the bolt cutters than Lutz had had with the hacksaw. Lutz and Fred went to the radio to tell the 89 they needed some cutting torches, but received an immediate nix. Meanwhile, David, back at the reel, with the bolt cutters and what was left of the good hacksaw blades, cut through a cable section.

Coast Guard cutter 44304 arrived at 2:00 and remained on standby. None of the men on board the *Fargo* noticed its presence.

David and Fred cut and cut and cut the cables a section at a time... and unraveled, unraveled, and unraveled them. Nonstop. It took 10 minutes to cut Larry from the lines, shedding parts of the net as they went. Dick's body became exposed. Although still entangled, it was apparent his back was arched against the reel and he was all but decapitated. Meanwhile, Lutz readied the Stokes litter. He undid the straps, laid the blankets so they could wrap Larry in them. MacGillis helped with the removal of the cable segments.

"He's out! We got him!" It was 2:08 as David and Fred cut the last of the tangled cables that had bound Larry.

Lutz and MacGillis supported the exhausted, injured, semiconscious, and dying man who collapsed into their arms as soon as he was released.

The four lifted Larry onto the Stokes litter. Lutz and MacGillis wrapped and secured him. While trapped in the cable, Larry had not allowed himself to urinate. He knew that would only make him wetter and colder. As Lutz and MacGillis tightened the last strap across his abdomen, for the first time in almost two days, as Larry put it, "I pissed all over!" Although embarrassed, he also didn't care. He was alive, elated to be found, rescued, and freed. Elated not to be alone.

The 1489 came back in for the hoist and Lutz secured the lines to the litter.

Lutz radioed, "Secure! Up, up, up!"

The litter lifted off the deck as the two Coasties guided its edges to ensure it went through the rigging without incident. David watched the ascent begin, slapped his thigh and yelped, "All right! Larry's on his way to the hospital!" Ever so slowly to avoid the danger of the Stokes litter spinning, the flight mechanic maneuvered the litter up to and through the door into the helo. It was now 2:18.

As the litter ascended, the men on deck, each and together, gathered in their strength and returned to the net reel to continue to work on releasing Dick's body from the remaining four wraps. To encase Dick so profoundly but not Larry, the net probably had started around the reel and Larry was just damn lucky his wish came true—*If only the net'll fall over the flange on that side of the winch....* He realized how few seconds close he came to death in that moment and, initially at least, was grateful for it. With part of Dick between the bottom of the reel and the deck, the job was not easily completed standing up. As with Larry, David and Fred took charge of cutting Dick loose, but it turned a gut-wrenching scene for all when they fully saw his head. As David commented "His...it was hanging by just some very little tissue. Here was a man who was my crewman."

His body was so contorted, MacGillis was right: Almost every bone in his body was broken. Whiddon was right: His back must have been broken. Larry was right: Dick was mush. As they cut the cable and net, Fred noticed one of Dick's gloves was caught securely in the cable line, the probable cause of what had pulled him over the reel.

They cut more cable and net loose. Suddenly, the weight of the fish began to unfurl the net from the reel. Dick's body landed on the deck. Net and cable flopped, whipped, and slapped across the deck threatening to strike or lash overboard John, George, David, or Fred. These four men found their own lives in danger as a cable end slammed the deck inches from one man then another. It lashed the air above their heads or beside their shoulders in those moments until one of them was able to reach and lock the gear and winch. Each man then quickly looked around to be sure all were on deck and standing. No one said a word. They just assessed the status of the others, realizing how close they'd come to further disaster.

Lutz looked up, either hearing the helicopter or thanking God they were still alive. He saw the 1489 was still on scene.

David and Lutz had the same thought, David saying. "Tell them to get my brother-in-law to the hospital. He needs medical attention *now*. This other man's all but decapitated. Time doesn't matter for Dick."

Lutz radioed the helo. "The second man's already dead. Don't worry about him. Go!" He went to the gunwale and vomited into the sea. The 89 departed for Tillamook at 2:21.

Larry, on his arrival in the helo, said to the crew, "At least you guys speak English! I don't have to teach you!" He chuckled, thinking about the bears that'd been on the boat with him.

His rescuers exchanged a glance that, if they understood him correctly, indicated they thought he had gone over the edge. Aware enough to notice the glances, Larry decided to stick to commenting on how cold he was, how warm he felt now. In addition to his first comments about speaking English, he also spoke in rapid, broken sentences, and his swollen lips and tongue further garbled his speech. The crew found him incoherent. As mentioned earlier, hallucinations have a reason for occurring. To survive, Larry needed the leprechaun and bears. If the crew understood his isolated words, the flight mechanic, Dr. Barnes, and the other crew just weren't in on the reason for the mention of bears. Trained as they were to rescue, they probably had no personal experience of hallucinations or surviving and fighting for one's life in a dangerous and extreme situation.

Larry had never been in a helicopter before. He felt safe and was beginning to feel warm on a ride to life that had a different kind of movement from a boat at sea, and Larry found the helo shook like hell. His body temperature had probably fallen into the 80s. By all rights, he should have been dead, but all he knew was he "was really, really cold." Now, almost incredibly, he was a happy man who could finally sleep and lapse into moments of unconsciousness and incoherence as Barnes pumped warm air into his lungs.

Larry's clothes under his Helly Hansen jacket were soaked. In the next 10 minutes, the doctor, flight mechanic, and avionics man cut away his jacket, Hickory shirt, and Duofold top. Larry's joy contrasted with the guardsmen's appall. Moore, amazed he was still alive, looked at Larry. He saw his left arm clearly, an image he retains to this day. "His left forearm looked as if it were made of clay. The cable was put into clay and taken back out again. It was a perfect impression of the cable." Moore's view was the image Larry had foreseen the moment the cable first grabbed him. Moore, like David, assumed Larry would lose his fingers, at minimum, and probably his arms. Years later, Moore said this was one of the rescues discussed when pilots sat around and reminisced about the unusual cases.

The three men in the back wrapped him in a thermal blanket. Barnes could not find his blood pressure so he did an estimate based on palpitations. Larry's palp blood pressure was 80 and his body temperature about 85 degrees, both very dangerously low.

As the 1489 transported Larry over the Garibaldi Bar, down Tillamook Bay to Tillamook Hospital, the main task of the doctor was to keep Larry warm, conscious, and breathing. If anything, the lack of circulation in his arms, the severe frostbite in his feet, and his blackened legs kept the cooled blood in his extremities from returning to his heart and causing a heart attack. So ecstatic to be rescued, Larry's primary thought was not his life or excruciating pain but his joy at being alive and with human companionship.

"Talk to me. Talk to me," one of them said. "What's your name?"

"Larry Hills," he mumbled.

"How old are you?"

"Thirty-four."

"Married?"

"Yeah."

"Kids?"

"Yeah."

"How old?"

"Seven. You speak English," Larry smiled and dozed off.

"What's the name of your boat?"

"*Fargo*."

"What were you doing?"

"Last load…. The last load." Barnes shook his head at that response. Any time Larry seemed to doze off, Barnes or the flight mechanic asked him questions. It didn't matter they couldn't understand his words. They just kept him mumbling all the way to Garibaldi.

Except for necessary communication to Astoria, Whiddon and Moore flew silently toward shore.

Once Larry was on his way to Tillamook, David, Fred, John, and George stood momentarily numb and exhausted, staring at the gray sea, sky, and boat, but each saw only Larry and Dick in images rimmed by emotion.

When David finally broke the silence, the three men looked at him.

"He crewed for me four months last summer, tuna fishing off Southern California."

Solemnly they placed Dick's body in a deck checker, a trawler's deck compartment with sides a foot tall, designed to hold the different species of fish when sorting.

Respectfully they stood. Lutz and MacGillis wore their Coast Guard mustang suits. The fishermen stood in their Helly Hanson dark olive green rain gear. Four men at an impromptu funeral where their vocations happened to place them. Spray, blown by the now 20- to 35-knot February winds on the North Pacific, continued to wash over them and the deck.

As they stood, the 44-foot cutter radioed on the VHF. "USCG 44304 calling *FV Fargo*. USCG 44304 calling *FV Fargo*."

David went into the wheelhouse. "*FV Fargo* here."

"We're coming over to tow you in."

"We're ready."

David walked out to announce, "They're towing us in to Garibaldi."

Concerned about the seas washing the body overboard, someone from the 44 suggested putting Dick's body in the cabin.

"No. I can't. Can't do that," said David. He's a good friend of mine. Was." Fred couldn't stomach that thought either. With the slick deck, gear in the way, and waves breaking over the sides, Lutz radioed back that he declined to solo that task.

After its 25-minute wait, the 44-footer moved in; a new chore greeted the four wet and chilled men. After brief nods across the water, the cutter had its stern alongside the *Fargo*'s bow. The crew threw the monkey's fist, the knot at the end of the heaving line attached to the double-braided Samson towline, to the *Fargo*. MacGillis, with Vandecoevering's help, fastened this towline to the *Fargo*'s bow cleat.

It paid out from the figure eights on the deck of the cutter until it reached the proper length to stretch from crest to crest and alternatively trough to trough without whipping; the stability of the towline depended on this. The remainder of towline the cutter's crew wound back onto the drum. At 2:33, it headed for Tillamook Bay with the *Fargo* in tow. The Garibaldi Bar now had 20-foot breakers on it. Not only would no sensible seaman cross a bar like that, he certainly would not do so when towing a disabled vessel. Further, it would soon be dark. David went to the wheelhouse.

"*Fargo* calling cutter 44304."

"44304 here."

"Do not tow us across this. I've been crossing this bar all my life and I wouldn't even cross it alone right now, let alone with a tow."

"Agreed. We can go back out and wait on the tide."

"Could. But a change in tide does not guarantee safe passage over this bar," replied David who had crossed this bar probably more times than all these Station Tillamook Bay Coast Guard boatmen put together.

"Agreed. I'll get back to you shortly."

After brief discussions between Station Tillamook Bay and Station Astoria, at the mouth of the Columbia River, the 44304 called the *Fargo*. So dangerous was the Garibaldi Bar right now—winds 20 to 35 knots; seas 12 to 15 feet; and the bar's breakers 20 feet—at 4:15, the station closed it to all traffic. The 44 and the *Fargo* were on their way to Station Astoria at Cape Disappointment, 50 miles north. It was going to be a long night and a rough ride for all on both boats.

None of the four men was happy with that. Still numb from emotional and physical exhaustion, they had looked forward to getting into port at Garibaldi. Instead, once again they stood dazed.

For two days the doors had hung from the galley posts unfastened, clanging their incessant port and starboard. David and Fred fastened and firmed the doors to one another high across the deck. The banging ceased. To give a smoother ride to the mouth of the Columbia, they let down the stabilizers, the long arms with submerged finned counterweights that provide stability to a boat when hauling net over the side, dead in the water, or in rough seas.

Their work completed, the men went inside the galley and sat at the table. They were spent and chilled to the bone. It felt good to be out of the wind, spray, and rain. Wet and cold from the experience, David and Fred removed their rain gear and donned the two survival suits David found stored in the unused head.

Lutz and MacGillis sat in their mustang suits, the Mac-10 Coast Guard flight suits—orange flotation coveralls that zipped crotch to throat, with Velcro snaps at the wrists and ankles, topped by a vest that doubled as a life preserver and had a signal mirror, flare, radio, and airbags in the pockets. Even out of the wind and rain, MacGillis, wet beneath his suit, never did warm up. Periodically, he went into Larry's stateroom and laid under one of Larry's sleeping bags. Lutz remained chilled also. The men sat at the table for the long ride to Astoria, numb and exhausted by the events they had witnessed and experienced. It was a bad case for Lutz and MacGillis, for MacGillis, his first rescue handling a dead man, for Lutz, only his second. For David, the sadness and shock of losing his buddy began to overwhelm him. It was too soon to let go of the person and friendship. He sat, deeply pained at Dick being outside in the deck checker. He finally went to his bunk and took his sleeping bag out and covered him with it. George walked out with him. Cold water splashing on Dick made both his friend, David, and the stranger, George, feel uncomfortable. They wanted to protect him, help him. They felt a sense of guilt at being relatively warm while Dick was out in the almost freezing, wet ocean spray. On the long journey, they occasionally continued to check on him.

I want to comfort you. It's a personal thing. Dick, you're my friend. Here we are inside the boat trying to stay warm, and you're out getting that cold wake on you. Damn it.

David shuddered.

Back inside, he still saw him.... *Nasty weather and you're getting rolled around in that checker. I gotta go back out. Maybe I should kind of relocate you, Dick. What I want.... Here I'm nice and warm in a survival suit and you're...cold.*

Infrequently, the men pulled themselves from silence to single-sentence conjectures.

"What happened?"

"Dick got his glove caught in the line. Pinched it."

"Pulled him over?"

"Had to."

"Larry went under the line. Boat rolled a bit and he reached up and grabbed it."

"Or over it."

"Over it. Oh. Yeah, over it."

"Think he'll lose his fingers?"

"Or his hands."

"Or his arms."

No one mentioned that he'd never fish again. None dared think about whether or not he would survive his injuries; after all, they had just saved his life.

Unneeded now, their adrenaline surges dissipated across the next couple of hours. Their sadness grew, as if a fifth man had arrived in the quarters of the wheelhouse.

Three-fourths of the earth's surface is ocean. Only a handful of fishermen and researchers know any small portion of it intimately. David knew these fishing grounds as well as his back yard. When they were over the reef where no one fished, he went out on the stern deck to release to the ocean floor the net full of the two-day dead and now useless fish. He ran the net out fully, then cut the remainder from its reel fastenings. He did not want fishermen to snag it and ruin their gear.

As they neared the Columbia River Bar, a Cape Disappointment 52-footer, the *Triumph*, came out to meet them. One of the men on board was Jim Bankson, 20 years later to be the master chief's boson's mate at Station Tillamook Bay in Garibaldi.

"It was an ugly call. At Columbia River Bar there was bad weather and big swells. I was not surprised they could not tow it over the Garibaldi Bar." The Columbia River Bar, now classed as the world's most dangerous, on this February day, had only 8- to 10-foot breakers and was less dangerous than Garibaldi's 20-foot breakers. The *Triumph* tied itself alongside the *Fargo* to provide additional stability as the three vessels crossed in tandem, thus giving the best control to cross the bar and fasten to the dock at 12:30 a.m.

David and Fred took the offered coffee inside the Station and called their wives to come get them. By the time Denise Vandecoevering and Karen Hamann arrived, David received a call from his family saying Larry would be on his way to Portland at first light. The two couples drove the 50 miles down the coast to Garibaldi arriving before dawn.

The repercussions of dealing with death or post-traumatic stress come in intervals. A person deals with the event at the time or the repercussions come back later usually at two-, five-, or 20-year intervals. Although shaken to the core by Dick's death, David seemed to have dealt with that at the time. One way he may have done that was to cut him loose and then remain with him, letting his emotions have their way for the duration of the voyage. David had been with Dick for about 11 hours, not in the traditional manner of a wake, but he had held his own private one. However, Lorraine Vandecoevering, David's mother, said David had flashbacks about the scene for several years afterward.

Dick Cooley's funeral was held Tuesday, Feb. 16. One of the songs at his service was the Eagles' "Desperado," one of his favorites. He was 30 years old and had worked as a mill worker and a commercial fisherman.

The obituary listed his father, William F. Cooley, his stepmother and mother, two sons, Joey, age 6, and Billy, age 4, as surviving him in addition to his three step siblings. Dick's pallbearers included David Vandecoevering, Rodney Hamann, Mickey Orr, and Dan Fisher.

Dick's obituary made no mention of the fatal shooting of his brother, his only sibling, some 18 years earlier. His brother, William F. Cooley, Jr., was in a car with his girlfriend and another couple when they went down a road, stopped at a gate, realized their error and intended to back up. A guard came out and when William Cooley, Jr. got out of the car to tell the guard their error and intentions, the guard shot him in the chest, twice, killing him instantly. Bill Cooley was now left with two grandsons and no sons, yet everyone interviewed 21 to 25 years later, stated that Dick had only one son, Billy, until he, now known as Will for half his life, stopped by Lorraine Vandecoevering's house a month after his 30th birthday. He said Joey was his halfbrother and Dick's stepson whom Dick took in as his own.

PART V

MENDING

Fishermen remove their rings before going out to sea as a
precaution against getting their fingers ripped off by the gear.
Larry was not wearing his wedding ring at the time
of his accident, but even so, he was now married to me more
than ever. In sickness and in health, till death do us part.

Bev Hills

I still have this streak [of stubbornness] in me, but it has been
eroded over time by the sands of compromise necessary to
maintain marital bliss.

Larry Hills

As the Coast Guard 44-footer fastened its lines to the disabled *Fargo* 12 miles out at sea, two emergency medical technicians watched intently as the helicopter approached for a landing, its mechanical burring growing louder and louder until it hovered overhead, then set down. The technicians ran across the tarmac with the gurney as the whoop slowed. If asked, they would not have noticed the change as the rotor blades began to idle; however, these changes were action signals to them. Whiddon left the engine running as the three crew in the back opened the door and readied the Stokes litter. Gurney at the helo door, the five men lifted the litter onto it.

"Larry Hills. Temperature 85 when we got him in the helo," Dr. Barnes stated.

One of the technicians exhaled loudly and glanced at him in recognition of the statement. The other technician simply repeated, "85."

"Estimated blood pressure is 80," Barnes continued. Larry's systolic and diastolic blood pressure so weak as to be unreadable, Barnes was able to find the systolic only by feeling the heart's palpations. With 80 as the top or palp number, a person is close to passing out.

"Palp BP 80." One of the technicians frowned. "Pulse?"

"Pulse 92."

The litter secured, the technicians, Barnes, and an enlisted Coastie rushed a semi-conscious Larry to the ER. The doors flung open and a young Dr. Mohr, on call that afternoon, greeted them.

"His body temperature was 85 when we got him in the helicopter. His pulse 92, but I couldn't get any blood pressure reading. Palp BP is 80."

Dr. Mohr repeated, "Body temp 85, pulse 92, palp 80, no BP."

Mohr took Larry's pulse, now at 90 and regular, and noted the time, 2:40. His body temperature had climbed to 89 degrees. Mohr could not obtain regular blood pressure either.

The two Coast Guardsmen jogged back to the helo with the litter. Dr. Barnes, an overweight National Health Services doctor working in the Coast Guard, walked back. Within the minute, low on fuel, the helo whirred up and off to Astoria.

As the nurses stripped and cut off what clothes the Coast Guard had not removed, and covered him with a heat blanket, Mohr asked Larry his name.

"Larry Hills. And I'm warm," he slurred across his blistered lips and tongue, both large and blackened from the salt and exposure. He smiled, or so he thought, at being in a building on this cold February day.

Mohr looked at his arms, mangled and imprinted with the depression marks of the cable, the indentations that had struck Moore so vividly less than a half hour earlier. He noted some of the tissue inside his patient's forearms was black. Decomposition had started. His face was dark from exposure, his lips and inside his mouth covered with black blisters. Mohr questioned whether Larry would survive.

He inserted an intravenous catheter in his upper chest to give life-saving medication and fluids — 17 liters in 17 hours. Larry's pulse, body temperature, and blood pressure stabilized across these first hours, but the damage was done. When Mohr inserted the Foley catheter, the scant amount of urine that emerged was black and thick. Larry's kidneys had shut down due to decreased fluid flowing to them. He had had no water for two days. In addition, his arms were compacted and crushed in a vise. With blood vessels compromised and dead-ended, fluid build-up started immediately. Called compartment syndrome, what fluid there was in his body leaked into and remained in the severely damaged tissues of his arms without circulating through his heart, organs, or extremities. His arms swelled when the fluid had nowhere to go and formed pockets. His hypothermia, key to keeping him alive on the vessel, now threatened his life.

So great ballooned the swelling, it splinted his fractured left wrist and his chipped, dislocated right elbow. Blisters on his lower arms, hands, and fingers grew to the size of almonds, apples and cantaloupes. He had emphysema, specific to having been upside down for at least 24 hours, and was developing cardiac dysrhythmia. His greatest danger, however, remained kidney failure, the result of his crush injuries, dehydration, and decreased blood pressure.

By 4:00, an hour and a half after admission, his blood pressure finally registered at 82/60 and his body temperature had risen to 92.6 degrees. The Tillamook hospital staff described him as alert and cooperative. He was so happy to be warm, it would be months before he wondered about his survival, hands, or his fishing career.

After Mary dressed Bev, she helped her walk to the kitchen and sat her down. Bev blinked at the bright florescent lights. She was still so drugged that the blue floral wallpaper she had hung in her sister's kitchen was only a haze.

"Come on, Bev. Wake up. Drink your coffee," Mary encouraged as the two of them sat at the island in her kitchen.

"I'm tryin." Between sips of coffee, Bev felt dizzy as she tried to escape the fog of the sleeping pill and her own profound psychological shock. But her head drooped again as she dozed off.

The phone rang. It was their father, Larry Vandecoevering.

"Larry's being helicoptered in. He's alive but he might not make it."

"Uh," stuttered Mary. "I don't want to say that."

"Of course not."

"Your mother and I will call his folks once we know he's in the hospital and stable."

"OK."

"How's Bev?"

"Waking up. We're going to go to the hospital shortly. OK, bye."

In another attempt to get her to awaken more quickly and fully, Mary offered, "Let's go see Larry." She reached out and rubbed Bev's hand and arm.

"I just want to touch his face one more time. See him. Touch him. He's not at the bottom of the sea. He's not at the bottom of the sea." The weight of perpetual gloom lifted from her and she saw a dawn for what seemed like the first time in her life.

"You're going to be able to touch his face, Bev. As soon as you can stand, we'll go to the hospital. But you have to be able to walk to the car and into the hospital. I'm trying to get you ready." Just as people talking more loudly to a blind person, Mary tried to cram the air space with words as if that would help Bev wake faster and make Larry heal more quickly. Make everything better, back to normal. "Let's get up and walk."

Bev was unsteady on her feet and her knees occasionally buckled from drug-induced exhaustion, but with Mary's help she made it to the far end of the living room. Back to the island. The living room. The island. Mary sat her down, picked up the mug to get Bev her third cup of coffee in less than an hour. The light was beginning to fade as evening approached. Bev had taken the sleeping pill 24 hours earlier and Mary was now feeling an even stronger urgency to drive her to the hospital.

"I wanna see Larry." After drinking half of a third mug, Bev's attempt at normal speech still slurred as if she were drunk.

"Are you ready? Let's try walking to the living room again."

She was still a bit unsteady, but her knees didn't buckle and she leaned on Mary just once this time.

"Sit down and finish your coffee and then we'll go."

On the 20-minute drive from Garibaldi to the Tillamook Hospital, Bev dozed off intermittently.

"Is that rain?" she asked.

"It's fog. Misting."

"I'm gonna see Larry. I'm gonna see Larry," Bev whispered as a chant, then almost shouted, "Mary! I'm going to see Larry!"

"Yeah, Bev! We're going to go see Larry!"

"My wish comes true," Bev whispered softly.

"What?"

"Oh. Nothing."

"Just like when we were kids? 'Oh, nothing,'" Mary teased.

Bev's laugh made Mary feel better and a broad smile crossed her face for the first time in two days. She glanced over at Bev who sat there beaming and with tears streaming down her cheeks.

As they pulled into the parking lot by the ER, Bev began a chorus of "Oh God. Oh God. Thank you. Thank you. Drive me to the door. Drive me to the door, Mary. Let me out, let me out." Bev grabbed the door handle and jerked it.

"Bev! Hold it. I'm parking right now. We're as close to the ER as I can get."

Bev was out of the car before Mary had the key out of the ignition. Because of her own stress, she didn't pull the key out straight and it seemed to stick. "Oh the heck with it," she said as she rushed out of the car after Bev, not even shutting the door tightly. It's not raining that hard, she thought.

At the ER entrance, a small group of reporters started asking Bev questions. She stared at them as if they were bizarre events out of another time and place. Mary caught up with her. "Come on, Bev. In we go."

"Where's Larry?" Bev demanded.

"We're here to see Larry Hills," Mary said. By this time, everyone in the hospital knew who and where Larry was.

"Follow me," someone said.

Without so much as a hello to Dr. Mohr, Bev walked up to Larry. Mohr and the nurses looked up and paused briefly.

Bev reached out and touched his face with a hand full of care and love. *Touched his face!* She stared at his arms and hands—two huge blisters the size of cantaloupes nested among the multitude of smaller ones. She saw his swollen face, blackened tongue and lips, fingers and legs. She looked at his feet, black as their wood stove. She saw the love of her life, the father of her child. He was not at the bottom of the sea and she trembled as her joy welled to tears. His eyes flickered in recognition of his beautiful wife.

Oh, God! She thought, shocked and aghast. *He looks awful.*

"Aw Bev. I held it just fine till they put me in the basket and someone pushed on my bladder and I pissed all over myself. I'm so embarrassed."

"It's OK," she responded, vaguely wondering why he worried about such a trivial thing.

Part of her wanted to stand there and look at her husband all day. Part of her wanted never to see what she saw. She stayed with him for less than five minutes, but her one wish—to see Larry one more time, to touch his face—had come true. She thanked Mohr, and turned to leave with her sister.

When they walked out of the hospital, the winter afternoon had grown dark. Still there, the reporters again fired questions at Bev. She winced at their invasion of her privacy.

"How is he doing?"

"Leave me alone."

"Is he going to survive?"

No longer considering that possibility, she felt socked in the stomach.

"I don't have anything to say to you."

"What happened on the boat?"

"Go to hell!" she said severely.

Bev didn't know what was going on. She didn't want to think he still might not make it. She had had no time to sit down and think about anything. Her head was swimming, and it would be days before it was clear of the effects of the sleeping pill, and weeks before the extent and reality of Larry's injuries soaked in. Reporters in her face were the last thing she needed.

By evening, Portland television and radio began to broadcast the news across Oregon. Larry was a known figure, not only in the Northern California and Oregon fishing world, but also in Lake County, 400 miles southeast of Portland where he and Bev had lived in Paisley and Lakeview. Local Lake County residents heard it on the news. One rancher friend of Larry's learned of the accident when he saw the rescue mentioned on a national news program the next morning.

In the dark, early hours of Friday morning, Mohr called Bev to tell her Larry needed to go to Good Samaritan Hospital in Portland. Due to the renewed storm, an ambulance, not a helicopter, would transport him. She was to ride in the back with Larry. Mohr anticipated the ambulance would leave about 6:00 in the morning. Mary took her back to the hospital. The ambulance drove the fog-shrouded Coastal Mountain Range's two-lane road that remains to this day one of narrow shoulders and steep curves. Sitting in the ambulance, Bev returned to what her whole self cried out for: Her thrill at being with Larry. She reached out and laid her palm tenderly against his face.

He's alive, she thought. Conscious, sort of. That he didn't talk to her didn't matter. He occasionally looked into her eyes and that made tears of joy well in hers. The EMTs kept checking his vital signs, oxygen and IV tubes, monitoring his life. The 90-mile ride seemed to take an impossibly long time: Bev and the ambulance crew knew his life balanced on a filament. Riding behind the ambulance was Bev's brother-in-law, Dave Jordan, also a fisherman. He stood at the ER entrance of

Portland's Good Samaritan waiting for his sister to get out. Newspaper, radio, and TV reporters also waited.

"Mrs. Hills, how's your husband?"

"How badly injured is he?"

"Was he conscious on the ride up?"

She whipped her head around to see who spoke and stared at a group of reporters.

"Leave me *alone!*" she spat out.

Dave, trying to protect his sister-in-law, said, "Get out of here. You're not helping the situation at all." He put his arm around Bev and ushered her through the emergency doors after Larry's stretcher. She was in tears.

On arrival at Good Samaritan, Larry was soon in ICU. His temperature was normal, his pulse 80 to 90 and regular. His blood pressure, taken by the femoral artery this time was 210/100.

Bev, still numb from the events of the previous three days and the lingering effects of the sleeping pill, could not hear the medical staff as they talked to her. She did not even see the mime quality of mouths opening and closing with information. Someone explained seven forms to her. She signed them all, thus giving permission for catheters and surgeries.

Good Samaritan doctors found the toes and the soles of Larry's feet dark purple and swollen, the discoloration and swelling continuing up to his knees. He already had necrotic tissue on his hands, arms, and feet. Now gone were the cable impress marks that Lt. j.g. Moore and Dr. Mohr had seen. Blisters still covered his swollen fingers, hands, and arms.

Larry had rhabdomyolysis, a breakdown of muscle fibers. Their cellular contents now leaked into his circulatory system. First described in crush injury victims during London's 1940-1941 bombing raids, rhabdomyolysis also causes the release of dangerous amounts of potassium, phosphate, and sulfate into the system. While these chemical elements belong in cellular structure, when they circulate through the body in high concentrations, they poison it. Acute renal failure results. According to Jewett, one of the doctors who was soon to treat him, Larry was in renal failure "due to toxic effects on the kidneys from dead muscle in his arms as well as his prolonged exposure prior to rescue." In spite of this toxicity in his system, hospital staff found him "totally oriented, fully responsive, easily communicative, and complaining of moderate distress at rest and severe pain when his arms are moved." By Friday when his body temperature finally became normal, Larry still felt hypothermic. He continued to shiver uncontrollably for days and his teeth chattered as he complained of feeling very cold.

The instant Larry's hand was caught by the cable line, Bev's life catapulted from being a doting mother and happily married young woman, to that of a distraught wife. She had experienced the blackness of grief picturing her husband snagged with his trawl net on the ocean floor, and even when it turned out he was alive, her life looked grim. She knew she could become a widow at any moment, or if not, then the nursemaid to a near-death quadriplegic, helpless as a baby.

Alone in a big city, flat broke, and without her little boy, she was desperately lonely. Unable to afford a motel and wanting to stay with Larry, she slept in the plastic chair in his ICU cubicle, eating off his tray. He lay on his back, pinned to the bed by pulleys and tubes, needles and monitors, his swaddled arms in cushioned slings suspended above his head, his elbows about 8 inches above the bed. Bev was his anchor, now a 24-hour nursemaid by his side in his 9-by-9 ICU glass cubicle. The lights remained on always. Through the glass walls, she listened to the noises of alarms, intercoms, and people wailing their death throes. Doctors and nurses came and went, examining and treating him. Confused, dizzy, and tumultuous, she reached to grapple with her new reality yet kept coming away empty-handed, empty-hearted.

His first care plan, on his day of admission—February 12—involved five doctors and the nursing staff. Typed single-spaced, it was four pages long and identified seven problem areas—necrosis secondary to the trauma and exposure, acute renal failure, hypothermia, a collapsed lung and emphysema caused by small sections of ruptured cells, his chipped and dislocated right elbow, his broken left wrist, and his psychological state.

Not only was he stunned by the trauma, he still had enough adrenaline coursing through his system that his body remained on high alert...*for three more days*. To keep his cubicle sterile, the door to his area remained closed. Larry, still fully conscious and in much pain, continued to hallucinate. The hallucinations were predictably intensified by the morphine he received. He occasionally yelled at Bev.

"Goddamn it, Bev! Tie the doors! Help me out of this! Why are you standing there?! Get David on the radio! *Do something!*"

Bev stared at him.

"You're so lazy! I'm gonna kill you when I get out of here."

Bev's images of him laughing, playing with Lincoln, lying open-eyed on the ocean floor, or in his cubicle yelling names and obscenities all jumbled uncontrollably inside her. Having him alive and yelling at her, even nonsensical things, made her burst into tears.

A few moments later, he asked her to move his ice pack. When she did, he got tears in his eyes and said, "Aw Bev, thank you. You're so kind to me. I'm so lucky to be married to you."

As if that were the kindest thing she'd ever done for him. Back and forth these moments came and went. It was a German nurse who helped her through these tough and conflicting events.

"It's the morphine, Bev. He's not mad at you. He doesn't hate you." This older woman knew of what she spoke both professionally and personally: She had just lost her husband to cancer. Larry bellowed insults not only at Bev but also at the German nurse, and anyone else who came by.

Tubes and wires, connected to various monitors and the dialysis machine, fastened Larry to the bed. He lay motionless yet still rocking back and forth on the disabled *Fargo*, still tied to the net reel. His hell had not abated.

In the first three days in the hospital, phlebotomists drew his blood and the lab ran results every two hours. By the second day, his body had stabilized sufficiently that he went to surgery for the first fasciotomy. The doctors opened his lower arms to expose the fascia, the nonelastic fibrous white sheet of tissue that encases or compartmentalizes the muscle. The muscles in Larry's lower arms, bound by the cables, had swollen under the stress of the lines and died due to lack of blood circulation, in spite of his meditative concentration on forcing blood through his arms. As the doctors suspected, the muscles were necrotic. They removed as little as necessary, hoping to save some forearm muscle in this first of many fasciotomies.

On Sunday, Feb. 14, the decrease in the swelling of his hands and fingers had not significantly improved, but that afternoon, Larry's five-day surge of adrenaline had run its course and he began to show signs of fatigue and sleepiness. Valentine's Day never crossed Bev's mind.

The next day, Dr. Estin, one of his first attending physicians, noted a slight decrease in the swelling of his fingers and palms. A blister the size of a tennis ball remained on his left palm. The overall swelling and a multitude of small weeping blisters some filled with fluid, some with blood, littered the layers of his skin midway to his upper arms. The large blisters that continued to his right upper arm stayed. Blisters still separated his fingers and covered his hands. Estin also noted that necrotic muscle tissue, so dark it was almost black, showed deep within the open wounds of both forearms. Larry's necrosis had continued and now worsened. He remained bloated, swollen, blackened, and in spite of his morphine drip, screaming in pain. His renal failure was still present.

By Tuesday—the day of Dick's funeral—Larry was still fighting for his life. His wounds leaked less, but new blisters continued to appear.

Oil stains, or perhaps dirt or dried blood, around his cuticles and beneath his fingernails reminded anyone, who had time to notice, this was a man who, down to the end, had earned his living working with his hands. His arms remained suspended. His kidneys still did not work...*and would not for 36 more days*.

Thursday, a week after his release from the lines, the second set of surgery photos showed a decrease in swelling but further darkening of the skin. The surgeons débrided more necrotic tissue from both his forearms. His toes remained black with no sensation—no warmth or chill, no pain. Although he was now eating, his psychological condition was rocky and he expressed great anxiety about the surgeries.

He told Bev one of the nurses had strung him up by ropes, suspended him on meat hooks and was spinning him around, dangling water in front of him.

"You gotta get me out of here, Bev. I can't take their torturing me any longer."

She assured him no one was torturing him. He lay there, silent.

"Another hallucination?"

"Yes, honey, it is. You're in bed. In the hospital. In Portland. You're not on the *Fargo* anymore. You're safe. Your arms are up, but that's to keep the swelling down." Bev tried to speak slowly, but she was still so anxious, her words came out rapidly.

Bev, his mooring throughout his long hospitalization, spent the week catnapping in a plastic chair in his cubicle. While it was tough living in the hospital, she found the nursing staff as considerate of her as of Larry. They showed her where she could take showers. She developed one of those bad colds that comes every 10 years. She had a fever and this time, unusually, she hallucinated. In the midst of reading *Clan of the Cave Bear*, the book's actions entered her life as she dwelt in a cave during the cold winter days. The nursing staff looked the other way as she ordered a lot for Larry's meals then ate the extra food. They told her where the staff coffee pot was and not to worry about leaving money. Good, because she didn't have a quarter in her pocket.

Lincoln stayed with his Aunt Mary and Uncle Jim. David had Larry's three large dogs in addition to his own two. For the next several months, every time he drove around Garibaldi or to Portland, he had these five dogs in the back of his pickup. When one started barking, they all chimed in. Everyone in town knew when he was coming... and why he had the cacophonous chorus in the back. When he came to the ICU, he hung around the corner rather than coming in. Bev and Larry wondered why. David thought he couldn't go in, but everyone was so concerned with Larry, no one thought to ask him. After standing outside quietly, he'd return to his noisy pickup and head the 90 miles back home.

As with all his surgeries—skin grafts, nerve transplants, removal of frostbitten toes— Bev waited with Larry as he was prepped. Each time, she held his hand as they wheeled him up to the "medical personnel only" door, and kissed him goodbye with the fear that would be their last kiss. Each time she got the word Larry had recovered from the surgery and anesthesia, she was elated. A step and a half forward, one step back, it was slow going but things weren't getting worse.

Despite all the many minisurgeries to remove gangrenous tissue from his arms in the hope they could be saved, at the end of the second week the doctors determined amputation was necessary. This was the only way to be rid of the continuously dying muscle tissue. They discussed this with Larry, then approached Bev for the surgery release to amputate his arms just above the elbows. She cringed as she signed the release, as if it were her fault they were cutting off his arms. She knew Larry would hate her forever, never forgive her for that signature. She wept the entire time he was in the operating room, fearful he would not survive yet again. She tried to picture, if he did survive, what life married to a functioning quadriplegic would be like. She had been to the depths of despair thinking he was dead, felt the ecstasy of the simple hope he might be alive, then relished the pure joy of knowing he was alive. Now she hoped he'd survive through the surgery even though he would have no quality of life.

One of her happiest moments was when the doctors came to her in the surgery waiting room to tell her that, as they readied for the amputations, they rediagnosed on the spot and determined he could keep his arms. She gasped for air and wept with relief. What they would do instead was to keep the 8-inch wounds on his forearms open for daily débridements until there was nothing left but bones and skin. It was eight months later before the wounds finally closed. But he did not lose his arms. Larry's meditative concentration on forcing blood through his arms had finally paid off. To this day, she thanks the doctors in the surgery room for their courage in taking the course they did. Considering the infection he had in his system, they took a risk, a risk that turned out then and now to be the right decision.

Her new joy did not last long. Within hours, she was once again in chaos with seemingly infinite worries and fears. The ache of her loneliness for Lincoln was intolerable. Only the daily visits and support from friends and family, the love she knew Larry had for her, and the decision to keep his arms kept her going in those moments when she felt she couldn't handle anymore and was ready to fold, cry herself to sleep, and not wake up.

The débridements continued. Bev watched Larry's keen eyes watch the doctors remove, without anesthetic, the small white strings which had once been live nerves and the stinking brown mush that had once been muscle from the insides of his filleted-open arms.

On Friday, Feb. 19, Larry met Dick Badger for his first physical therapy session. The two men, about the same age with similar senses of humor, hit it off immediately. Dick found Larry "alert, well-oriented, and in surprisingly good spirits" but fading into occasional catnaps during the first visit. His hands calloused as any fisherman's hands would be, still had large blisters, and were "quite flexible," Dick noted as he had him do the range-of-motion exercises. Larry's water intake was highly restricted due to his continuing kidney failure. In spite of small sponge-like popsicles to suck on, Larry remained as thirsty as he had been during his entrapment. Now he had found a new person to try to manipulate in his attempts to get water to drink. One of his favorite tricks was to say he needed an ice pack on his head. As the ice melted, he'd shift his head around to catch the water dripping off his face. Or he might say he needed one on his shoulder, then turn to bite it open and suck the water out of it.

When Bev took breaks from tending to Larry's needs, she explored the hospital. For weeks, she walked all floors and every section. She knew all the stairwells and when she came to the door saying what floor it was, she knew which wards were on that level. She sat in every waiting area she found, sat there until people began to look at her wondering why she sat there so long and no one came to speak to her.

She daydreamed. *I put a straw in his mouth so he can get a drink. I spoon-feed him, temperature testing the food first. I wash his face. I constantly adjust his pillows to support his head, sides, or legs. I tape his IVs back down when they become loose. I adjust the cords, tubes, and wires that are attached to his body. I scratch the itchy spot on his nose. I hold him when he's asleep or awake screaming in his spasmodic or intense shocks of pain. I wipe the tears from his eyes.*

She paused. *My only purpose for living is to be here for Larry.* She looked around, not sure whether she'd just thought that or had said it aloud. The others in the waiting area continued to sit silently or talk in hushed voices. Not sure whether she was being ignored or had kept her thoughts to herself, she blushed, rose, and continued her walk.

She investigated the hospital's different buildings. She never ventured outside the complex though, until one day the German nurse handed her $5 and said, "Get out of here. Go *outside* and buy yourself some lunch." Bev left, walked the neighborhood, watched the people, watched and listened to the traffic, saw pansies and roses in this city where flowers always bloom. Smelled the fresh air. Ate lunch in a restaurant.

On one of her walks, a nurse, new to the case, came in to change the dressings on Larry's arms. As she unwound them, she rushed to the wastebasket and vomited. He watched her remove her gloves, wash her hands, and don new gloves. She unwound the rest of the dressings. When she looked for where she'd put the packet of new dressing, she rested her gloved hands on the bed rail. Turning to open the packet with gloves now no longer sterile, Larry bellowed at her, "Don't touch me till you get new gloves on!" She startled and he saw tears in her eyes. "New gloves," he repeated more calmly. "New gloves. I can't risk *any* infection," and coached her through the rest of the process.

Bev returned just as the nurse was leaving.

"Where the hell have you been?" he asked accusingly. "She was a mess."

"I just went for a walk up and down the stairs."

"Please don't leave me alone in this hellhole."

The rest of February and March proceeded slowly with various arm and foot surgeries, medication changes, and some rehabilitation. Across these days and weeks, Bev watched Larry watch his perfect strong fingers slowly curl in, turn into hard, cold talons. Hour after hour, still lying in bed, he would stare at his immobile hands, waiting for the numbness to leave, trying to force movement into his limbs with neither nerves or muscle.

Lincoln's Aunt Mary occasionally brought him to the hospital. He was 7, and bored. He ate tasteless hospital food and took lots of naps in the ICU waiting room. Other times he sat there, listening to conversations he did not understand between adults he'd never seen before and would never see again. On a good day, nursing staff would bring him a 60cc. syringe. Now that was living. A 7 year old with his own squirt gun and permission to use it indoors!

For a break, Bev came in and sat down on the couch next to him, escaping into the pleasure of his presence. She just looked at him, loved him silently, as he leaned into her.

"Mommy, it smells in here. Can we go for a walk?"

She was happy just to sit with him. "Sure, Honey. Where do you want to go?"

"Let's go to the kitchen and you can cook me a *good* dinner. I want to eat your food or Grandma's food. Nobody here knows how to cook." He looked at her, knowing the impossibility. He wanted to make her feel better, to smile at him.

It worked. "Come on. Let's go for a walk. Outside!"

Lincoln quickly grabbed his two full "squirt guns."

"Would you like me to carry one of those?" He handed it to her and they left hand in hand for a walk in the sunshine.

A third set of photographs, taken the end of February, showed Larry's arms, still gaping with the long, open wounds, thin from little muscle left, yet healing to the color of normal flesh. He no longer had any gangrene or infections in his arm wounds. The color had returned in his legs, but his toes remained black from the severe frostbite. Once again, the doctors tapped on his shriveled black feet to check for sensation. Any sensation. There was none. He continued on dialysis. His chest, lungs, and broken bones were healing well. Other life-threatening situations arose when the catheter in his neck cracked and clotted. Because it was under a dressing, no one noticed immediately and the wound became infected with staphylococcus. Later, he developed peritonitis in his abdomen. Bev watched in horror, first as the catheter site on his neck became red with infection, then in total fear as the flexible plastic tube from his abdomen to the dialysis machine became blocked with pus, and his stomach bloated like those of dead cows she'd seen rotting in the hot, desert sun. More medications in the IV tubes. More hallucinations.

Nurses and doctors in and out by the hour or less. Once again, it was days before anyone knew whether Larry was going to defy death this time as well.

Beginning long-term improvement, his boredom grew. He began to watch *Perry Mason* and the news each day. Fishermen came by to visit and brought copies of *Ocean* and *The National Fisherman*. When Bev held them for him to read, the print was too blurry to see. He asked her to read them to him, never telling her or the staff his vision was blurred. He didn't want there to be one more thing wrong with him. Flat on the bed with his arms still suspended, he lay there thinking of which jokes to tell which person. Fortunate to have a window in his cubicle, he could see the American flag waving atop the Burnside Bridge. One morning, a window washer appeared suspended on his scaffolding. While delighted to see a new person, Larry panicked and obsessed telling Bev to tell someone to get him off there before he fell.

An excellent example of respondent (Pavlovian) conditioning, Larry's fear of having water, even one drop, fall on him, affected him intensely for months. Post- traumatic stress disorder (PTSD), its roots in respondent conditioning, is the continued response to any trauma after the original event has ended. First scientifically observed by Pavlov in his lab dogs after a flood, he termed it "analogous to traumatic neurosis in man." Identified in people centuries ago—Homer wrote vivid descriptions of it in the Iliad—and labeled with various names during the Civil War, and World Wars I and II, the diagnosis of PTSD was first established for veterans of the Vietnam War in 1980. It is characterized by a person's spontaneous reliving of a situation, efforts to avoid issues related to the original event, and other intense and similar emotions and behaviors. If anyone spilled one drop of water on Larry, his body tremored and he yelled at the person to go away, or accused the nurse of torturing him intentionally.

As communities do at a time of crisis, the Garibaldi Chamber of

Commerce with the help of many volunteers held a fish dinner in mid-April and raised $3,500 for the Hills family suddenly cut off from their income yet with a dramatic increase in their expenses. Bev knew about the dinner. What she didn't learn until after the fact was that the local Coast Guard families, in addition to helping with the dinner, had emptied their freezers and cupboards to fill the Hills' kitchen.

Driving home for the first time a couple of weeks after the dinner, very homesick and desperately in need of some good sleep, she buried her fears of driving in the city and headed into Portland traffic for the 90-mile trip home. She knew if she could get to Barnes Road, she'd be able to get to the Sunset Highway and then the coast. She turned onto Barnes and a "road closed" sign confronted her. Her fear of city driving and exhaustion combined into hysteria. She pulled over, cried, screamed, and shook, a necessary outlet after two months of holding herself together, until she was exhausted. She napped there at the side of the road, awoke, and summoned enough courage to drive back into Portland to start the journey home all over again.

She arrived at the house late in the day. It was cold and quiet. Their cat, Kinky, was nowhere to be found. She knew the dogs were with someone in the family. Lincoln's little Star Wars toys were still on the floor where he'd left them before he went to school that Thursday in February. She split some firewood, started the wood stove, and warmed the house as she spent the evening getting clothes and other necessities together.

Lonely, sad, and scared, she went to bed, and cried into Larry's pillow. She didn't know if Lincoln, Larry, and she would ever be home together again. She didn't know if she'd have the physical strength to take care of her husband. She didn't know if she and Larry would ever make love again. Finally, she cried herself to sleep, a fitful one but her first in two months in a bed and not a plastic chair.

In the morning, she opened a cupboard.

Surprised, she called her parents. "Mom, who put this food in my cupboards?"

"The local Coast Guard families. Did you look in your freezer yet?"

"No."

"I'll stop over in a few minutes. Go look in your freezer."

Bev hung up, opened the freezer, burst into tears, slid down the side of it to sit on the floor sobbing at their generosity. They found him, saved his life, and then filled the Hills' cupboards and freezer. These people were not officers but enlisted, all had their own families to feed, yet they had gone to this expense and trouble. But worse, in her last interaction with the Coast Guard, she had yelled at and argued with the Station Chief. Oh so rude. Rewarded with such generosity, she wanted to curl up and hide. Yes! Hide under her freezer. She was still on the floor when her mother walked in.

Later, she called Larry's parents and Lincoln in Lakeview; all was as well as could be expected. She did an inventory of the pets. A neighbor had seen Kinky a few blocks away the day before yesterday. Her brother, Tony, now had the dogs on his farm. She threw her things in the car, gave the post office keys to her sister, Marge, locked the house again, and headed back to Portland.

On the way back, she consumed herself worrying about money. They now had no income. She knew she didn't have the skills to earn what Larry had been making, let alone pay the medical bills which were running into the hundreds of thousands of dollars. Rent was not going to be a problem as they rented from her parents. Social Security income of $130 a month would not start for yet another month. Larry was ineligible for worker's comp because he was a self-employed fisherman. She feared he'd never work again. She tried but could not imagine what their future would be.

But she did know Larry was waiting for her in his hospital bed in Portland.

She walked in the room as a tray of food arrived. She fed him, caught up on his personal needs, and slipped into the routine they had unconsciously developed. She continued with the basics: feeding, washing, rubbing his aching and immobile legs, stretching his numb, lifeless fingers, holding him during the prolonged periods of general deep pain and the short bursts of his violent pain.

The first time he sat up, he became extremely nauseous, almost vomiting. When able to sit up for a few minutes without feeling nauseous, she sponge-bathed him.

As Larry's PT progressed, it included therapy to his legs, neck and shoulders to keep his inactive muscles from atrophying. The psychologist noted that "he and his wife seem to have settled in for this chapter," probably meaning that Larry was losing his temper and yelling at people less often. He still received morphine every four hours.

Finally, on March 21, his kidneys kicked in and he was off dialysis. Now in stable condition, he was moved from ICU to the reconstructive surgery floor. The room had a window with a view of a brick wall and a sliver of the Willamette River and Burnside Bridge. He could have the lights turned down. He could ask for the door to be closed for privacy or open so he could hear the chatter of people at the nurse's station. His arms, still numb from his shoulders on down, remained swaddled in thick bandages, suspended in slings. It would be the end of April before he was out of the slings and could grasp things between these bandaged arms. Such simple activities lifted his spirits. A note in his chart the beginning of April commented that he was working hard on his own and in PT. He was learning to do some things for himself. This gave Bev more time to ponder private thoughts—thoughts about Larry, Lincoln, even other people and events. Larry, however, was getting even more restless and hell-bent to get well and out of the hospital.

Other than Bev, his best companion in his new room came in the form of a fly. Still flat on his back, this new addition to his life made him extremely happy.

"Bev!" he exclaimed the first time he saw it, "A living thing in this damn place that's not a doctor or a nurse!" He stared at the fly for hours like a behavioral entomologist. Had he such an inclination, he might have had Bev take notes on its behavior. He gave special instructions to the staff—nursing and housekeeping: "Leave my fly alone!" It buzzed around the room for about a week. He watched it, studied it, talked to it, grieved the day it died. Thus began a different respect for the life of all living creatures.

After one of the débridements done while he was in the reconstructive surgery ward, his head was in such a position that he had his first glimpse inside his forearms. He looked down into the wounds to see between the bones. He saw the back side of the skin on the other side. The doctors had removed his muscles and what he saw was not himself but the inside of the animals he has skinned on the ZX Ranch and the fish he had gutted on personal catches. His heart sank. He could no longer maintain his denial of the devastating extent of his injuries. Never would he be able to build up absent muscles. Never would he have the ability to commercial fish again. He'd be lucky if he could grasp anything or freely move his hands or arms. He plunged into a depression. His sense of humor left. He returned to yelling at nurses, therapists, Bev. His world had turned inside out again. The image of Orion sinking below the horizon just before dawn flashed before him and Larry knew it had risen and set for the last time.

Still in a black depression and feeling very sorry for himself, he waited at the elevator one day, an aide pushing his gurney. His comeuppance was about to arrive. The door opened and in they went. On the next floor down entered a patient on a gurney. His arms and legs had been amputated at the trunk. Flat on their backs, these two men made eye contact. Larry saw ultimate sorrow…this man did not want to be alive. That instant, Larry's self-pity ended. Like a doctor said, he had a million choices in life before the accident; now he was down to 700,000. It was going to be hard to sacrifice his independence, to learn to depend on people…but he still had 700,000 choices. He knew he'd never use them up.

David continued to visit. Getting increasingly more creative, he brought Larry's Australian shepherd, Willy, several times. Willy was hesitant at the automatic doors, but oh so happy with all the patting and admiration he received. His highlight was seeing Larry. He wagged his bobbed tail and sat down against the gurney. During conversation, he sometimes got up and went over to lie by David's feet.

"Hey! What are you doing with my dog, David? Willy! Get back over here." Willy opened an eye at his name but did not budge. The two men smiled.

On April 8, he and Bev took their first jaunt through the rose garden on the hospital's third floor balcony.

"Hot damn, we're *outside*!" Larry exclaimed. No more investigating the same hospital floors, nooks and crannies. As Bev wheeled his stretcher, he smelled, looked, and listened. Thrilled with the blue sky and fresh air, he had a childlike fascination with things of spring—Japanese maple and cherry trees, rose bushes, daffodils, pansies all in bloom, birds, butterflies. Oops, stairs, can't go there. A moth flew near and they paused to watch its lyrical flight. Over the intake of a hospital's ventilation duct, it lost its control and *zhoop!*, it was sucked into the vent.

"Awk!" he yelled loudly. "No! It just ate the moth. Bev, this is awful. See what mankind does. Life is terrible sometimes."

Shortly after arriving on the reconstructive surgery ward, the medical record noted his skin, peeling away from his feet, was "ivory white" and his toes "gun-metal grey." Nothing had been done to his feet while in ICU; the purpose there had been to stabilize his life until his kidneys functioned on their own. In April, the toes on Larry's left foot were amputated, and his right foot amputated to the metatarsus. Expanding the number of doctors involved, one of the surgeons asked Dr. Styles Jewett to examine Larry's right foot since it was not healing well. When Jewett came to look, as the good doctor he turned out to be, he gave Larry a complete physical. He ended his report with the gracious statement, "Thank you for asking me to see this interesting patient with many serious problems." Jewett would become and remain Larry's primary physician for the next five years. Rehabilitation to his hands resumed with increased activities and time up to four hours a day, but sensation did not return to either hand.

Bev continued to care for his daily needs. She put his page turner in his mouth and propped the book on his chest. She washed his face and hair, trimmed his hair and moustache. She held the telephone to his ear and wrote messages for him, fetched and held the urinal for him, continued to hold him when he cried out in spasmodic pain.

Larry now exercised with 2-pound weights attached to his ankles with Velcro. On his first attempt, he stood three times for about two minutes each. Each foot was heavily bandaged due to the recent amputations. He had only initial and minimal dizziness and was able to shift his weight from one foot to the other. He did shallow knee bends and walked several steps with no breakdown or redness on either foot. May 10, three months after the accident, Larry was transferred to the nearby Rehabilitation Institute of Oregon (RIO). His range of motion in his shoulders was limited, his manual dexterity questionable, and his standing and walking balance poor.

When he began to take showers, PTSD kicked in again. He could see the thermometer on the wall said the temperature was 107 degrees. He knew that was warm. It was ice water! He sat in the shower wheelchair shaking like a leaf in an autumn breeze. It would be the end of August before he could take a hot shower without shaking.

Once at RIO, Bev signed him out for various outings. With him in a wheelchair, they went to a Laundromat, walked a few blocks of various local neighborhoods, stopped at a restaurant, had a beer and sandwich in a local tavern, and once loaded the wheelchair into a cab and went to a movie at the Baghdad Theatre. In early June, Bev and Larry went to Pittock Mansion Park, high on a hill above Portland for a picnic to celebrate Lincoln's eighth birthday. Lincoln, now living with Larry's parents, C. B. and Norm in Lakeview, had plenty of hugs for each of his parents. He was missing a few more teeth, other teeth had grown in. His glasses needed cleaning. His jeans were too short. *But he's still my little towhead!* thought Bev. Other than very brief visits to ICU, this was the first time Lincoln had seen his father since he had tucked him into bed before leaving Feb. 9 on the last fishing trip. Larry wore hospital scrubs; his arms and feet were swaddled in bandages. Lincoln towered over his 6' 4" father sitting in the wheelchair. He sat in Larry's lap and hugged and kissed his dad. A poignant scene they created— Larry in his wheelchair, his fingers splinted and straightened with reverse knuckle benders, his mother, C. B., in her wheelchair because of rheumatoid arthritis. C. B. reminded Larry his accident was within days of the anniversary of his father's death, but he had not connected the coincidence of the two. Lincoln played with his three cousins along for the day as their mother sat with the adults. Bev and Norm, Larry's stepfather, helped their mates. Larry's soda can had a straw about 2 feet long and no one noticed when Bev fed him lunch. As they parted, Bev hid her tears but screamed inside as Lincoln kissed her and then Larry one last time before departing with his grandparents for the 8-hour drive back to Lakeview. It would be late summer before Lincoln joined his parents in Garibaldi.

From 1798 until 1981, six months before Larry's accident, American seamen had been provided medical care through the U.S. Public Health Service. In the era of Reagan cutbacks, this almost 200-year-old policy changed. Private vessel owners now became responsible for the medical care of their crew. In his report to the insurance company, Dr. Jewett stated the damage to Larry's feet would give him a partial yet permanent disability. His arm recovery was "totally unknown at this time. His current joint stiffness, muscle loss, and shortening would make return of function to the upper extremities only partial at best. The prognosis for his ever returning to active work requiring heavy manual labor is nil." He also stated his future was "cloudy at best."

Little did he know the stubbornness of the man he was treating! Stubbornness: unreasonable unyielding in quality or character; difficult to handle or manage. Both have negative connotations. But it was Larry's stubbornness, persistence, and determination that had kept him alive and would soon enable him, despite his lifetime bilateral foot, arm, and hand disabilities, to build a new career in the outdoors, on land this time.

His four-month hospitalization had included 18 doctors and at least 17 surgeries. When he left RIO, his condition was still far from stationary. He now walked with some assistance less than 50 feet, was slowly building strength and tolerance, but was discharged in an electric wheelchair. His upper extremities had begun to show nerve regeneration with tingling in his forearms and hands. However, he had now and for the rest of his life "severe contractures of his forearm and hand muscles." Jewett remained hopeful he would have more nerve regeneration in the upper extremities.

Larry's discharge summary noted 18 medical conditions on arrival Feb. 12, six of which remained on his rehabilitation discharge four months later: arm, hand, and foot injuries, resultant skin grafts, and phantom and real pain. He left RIO and Portland in his 200-pound, electric wheelchair with left hand drive, reverse knuckle benders to straighten his contracting fingers, and orthopedic shoes on order for when his feet were good enough to wear them, orders for outpatient physical therapy in Tillamook, and a vocational rehabilitation referral. Also loaded into the pickup he had last driven that Friday evening in February from his home to the docks were all the medicines, bandages for daily changes, and therapeutic devices he would need until his next visit to the Portland doctors in a few weeks.

Once home, Larry needed help with almost everything. He was

6 inches taller than Bev, but now weighed only 40 pounds more than she. Still, it was hard for her to move him from bed to wheelchair and wheelchair to bed, but she managed. And finally, they shut their bedroom door.

When Lincoln came home at the end of the summer, his presence was indispensable and his chores had changed. Even at his young age, he was now and ever after the family wood and kindling chopper. He fed the dogs and cat, also back home. Finally, thought Bev, everyone was home. Hurting but together again. Pure bliss.

An avid and excellent reader himself, Lincoln was now the person who went to the library for his father. Good. Just another way for him to check out more books for himself too. Another job was to stay at home with his father when Bev ran to the store and did other quick and necessary household errands.

Larry was able to put a little pressure on the heel of his left foot and could scoot himself around the house in a standard wheelchair. They kept the electric one in the garage for outdoor excursions. When Bev had lifted him into the big one, she'd Velcro his hand to the control and he'd go up the hill across the street to his in-laws or down to the docks to check out the fishing boats or see David, Tony, or Fred. He still wore scrubs, and had added a fedora, and a blanket on chilly days. Noticeable on these summer days, his once sea-tanned face and hands were now pale and colorless. Every day Bev flushed out the still-open wounds of his arms and feet, put Betadyne on them before bandaging them. She covered his toeless foot with a loose sock and put an Ace bandage on his half foot. She worried about how filthy the sock and bandage looked by the end of each day, splattered with mud from the wet streets on the coast, but Larry never gave it a care; he was happy to be out and about. He probably shocked a few summer tourists, but from the locals he mostly received just a, "Hey, Larry! How ya doin'?"

In spite of the aspects of normalcy, reality was sinking in for all three of them. Lincoln didn't like people staring at or commenting on his father. He was still just plain Dad on the inside and most of the outside, and these people were rude. Bev was worried about finances. Larry was dealing with being disabled for the rest of his life, what he would do, and how he would provide for his family. They eliminated what couldn't happen—Larry would not fish or have a job of manual labor. Bev could go to work but would not earn as much as Larry had. By the end of summer, they had made their decision.

They decided to move back to Paisley away from the damp ocean climate, peoples' stares, and the daily reminders of his fishing life and the reality he would never fish again. It was Bill and Mary Schreiber who drove them from Garibaldi to Paisley in the fall. It was October— windy, cold, and the leaves blew off the cottonwoods as Larry and his family arrived permanently back in the High Desert. He and Bev remained ignorant of the import of the second struggle for his life they had just endured, and the struggle they were about to enter for stability, career, and family. They continued to remain consumed only by the daily fight to live.

On May 3, three months after Dick and Larry's accident and a month before Larry's discharge from the hospital, Bev's brother-in-law, Dave Jordan, captaining the *Miss Lorraine*, was hauling back his last tow of the day. He had decided to pick up a bit early and anchor behind Cape Lookout to spend the night out of the wind. Tuned to Channel 19, the fishermen's channel, an hour before dark, came a call.

"MAYDAY. MAYDAY. MAYDAY. This is the *Fargo*. We're rolling over. Going down!" The skipper, Richard Bolliger, was out the wheelhouse door. The boat rolled and he and his deckhand, Petey King, were in the water. They had been double-rigged shrimping, one net off each side. With the first net and its doors in, there had been a natural list. Within seconds, they could feel the second net had pulled the boat beyond the 45-degree angle to a capsize.

The *Miss Lorraine* was several miles away. Had the men on the

Fargo had time to give their location, it still would have taken the Coast Guard at least an hour to get there. Dave looked over and saw only an outrigger pole sticking straight up. He knew immediately the *Fargo* was on its side.

Bringing in his catch, he heard the call on his deck speakers. He ran into the house and radioed, "I heard you Richard. I see you. We're coming to get you." But Richard never heard that. Richard and Petey were already in the water. While Richard was hollering, "I can't swim! I can't swim," Petey, his deckhand, watched his life from tricycle to trawling flash before him and knew he was a gonner. Startled and panicked, the wet and cold men crawled up on the *Fargo*'s smooth red keel, the fear of death pushing them to its top. They sat there in the 30-knot winds, bouncing around, watching the 4- to 6-foot wind chop on top of the 8- to 10-foot seas. They could do no more than hope someone had heard the call.

Dave received no response. He also radioed the Coast Guard, knowing that Richard had called on Channel 19, not 16. The Coast Guard said they would stand by.

Good I'm here, thought Dave. *He never got his location out. The Coast Guard wouldn't have known where to look.*

As he drew closer, Dave saw the red hull of the capsized *Fargo*. He flashed his lights at them. Richard smiled—he was really glad to see that. Help was close by.

Alongside, a few minutes later, Dave hollered, "You guys OK?"

"Yeah, but I don't know how to swim," shouted Richard. Neither man had had time to don his life vest.

"I'll go load my gear and come back." He planned to load his nets on deck for better maneuverability. This way he could turn any way he wanted, kick the boat in or out of gear, whatever it took to get the men safely on board without tangling in his own nets. It would take only minutes and then he wouldn't need to worry about the current moving the nets to hang like an anchor or taking them into the propeller, leaving him dead in the water. Suddenly a larger than normal wave came and washed both men off the keel. No time to pull in the nets, or even to cut them loose. His only shot at saving them was at hand. If the net got caught in the prop, so be it.

"OK Scott. We gotta go *now!*" he called to his deckhand. They jumped off the flying bridge onto the main deck as the boat drifted in the trough with a net hanging under the boat amidships. By a miracle of God, it did not snag in the wheel. Dave kicked the *Miss Lorraine* back into gear and turned into the waves, figured he'd deal with the nets later— even call the Coast Guard if he had to. Dave and Scott each grabbed a line and threw them toward the men from the *Fargo*. The *Fargo* lay still in the trough, not a good place to be with gear out and in rough seas. Petey grabbed his line and swam as Scott pulled it in and helped him aboard. Richard, a strong, stout guy with not a spare ounce of fat on him, went underwater. Under the boat. Dave pulled the line hand over hand, while Richard hand over handed his way up the line. Soon both men were on board, cold to the bone, teeth chattering, shivering, and barely able to talk, but they were safe from their jump, the 20 minutes on the keel, and five more minutes in the ocean. They showered, put on clean clothes that Dave and Scott provided, and crawled into sleeping bags as Dave turned his attention to getting his shrimp on board.

As the boat continued to drift in the trough, the port net hung straight down and the starboard one remained under the boat. Dave powered away from them, forcing them to the front of the *Miss Lorraine*. He dropped the starboard net 10 fathoms below the surface and away from the propeller. As he then propelled forward, the port net trailed behind the vessel. He brought the starboard one to the surface and hauled it in, then loaded the port gear as well. Now, over an hour later with both men and nets safely on board, he called the Coast Guard to say, "We're OK and headed in. Thanks for standing by." He turned the vessel toward Garibaldi and headed into home port.

Bud Smiley, the skipper of the *Desire*, came along to watch the

Fargo sink. He took a LORAN reading on it. Right in the middle of one of their fishing grounds, fishermen would want to know where it was so they didn't catch their gear in it. He silently watched the *Fargo* turn into a mirage as it slipped beneath the water, then gradually disappeared in the dark green and black depths of May's waters. *Good sinking. No one in the Vandecoevering, Hills, Cooley, or Fisher families is ever going to have to look at this boat again.*

It rests in the darksome weeds of the ocean floor off Oregon's northwest coast, its Gibson Girl and denim wallpapers still firmly attached. The waters of the Kuroshio current flow past the vessel, fish swim in and out of its parts unaware of anything but their safe haven, unaware of the human stories that inhabit its remains, unaware of Susan Cooley Hadley's lingering widow's words, "I curse the Fargo to the bottom of the sea."

PART VI

ON THE TRAIL

Thousands of tired, nerve-shaken

over-civilized people are beginning

to find out that going to the

mountains is going home, that

wildness is necessity, and that

mountain parks and reservations are

useful not only as fountains of timber

and irrigating rivers, but as fountains

of life.

John Muir, 1898

Chapter 1

Before Larry left the house one day in 1988, Bev folded and stuffed two socks into the toe of his right hiking boot. He slipped his foot in, then his left foot in the other one. She laced and tied them. She thought, not without some worry, about his being alone in the wilderness; all he thought about was hiking all day scouting routes to find the best trail locations. She put the sandwich she'd made in a plastic container, the cookies in another, and filled his water bottle.

In his blue jeans and with the deep scars on his forearms hidden by his long-sleeved cotton shirt, Larry, 6' 4" with sandy hair and a red beard, looped his backpack over his arm. "Come on, Willy," he hollered to his black and white Australian shepherd.

He opened the back of the pickup and Willy hopped in, front feet immediately on the sides of the bed, barking to anyone who did or didn't want to listen. Larry climbed behind the wheel and put his two clawed fists around the key to turn the ignition. He pulled out the seatbelt with his fisted hands, grabbed it in his teeth, then, again with his fists, fastened it into the other end. After putting the vehicle in gear, he crooked his gnarled fingers, atrophied and retracted toward his palms, over the steering wheel and headed for the hills. Thirty miles down the paved highway, he turned west on the dirt road that passed several ranches and headed through the sage hillsides. The road narrowed as he approached a forest of Ponderosa. Parking where the dirt road petered out, Willy jumped out, too impatient to wait for Larry. Larry leaned against the bed of the pickup and surveyed the area. He wanted to build a horse corral here, one where others with disabilities could mount and dismount, travel the steep Moss Pass Trail on horseback. This was his favorite spot in the Fremont Forest and he had big plans for this area, plans that would enable him to share it with anyone willing to go out in the wilderness for a day or two. As he stared at the Ponderosa he didn't see the red bark stand out from the black underneath. He missed the smell of the pines, the fresh spring sage, and wild roses just blooming. He didn't hear the Clark's nutcrackers, the ravens, or the cicadas as they told of the hot day coming. He saw the layout of the horse coral, outhouses, and the parking. He rearranged them, changed their size or angle in the still thickly-wooded landscape. He'd put it on paper some day when it poured or was over 100° and he was forced to work in his office.

Walking two miles uphill was easy on the hard-packed soil. It was June; the snow had melted and it hadn't rained for a couple of weeks. He looked down at the Chewaucan River snaking its way through the grass valley oasis in the middle of southeastern Oregon's High Desert. He daydreamed westward to the mountains of the Gearhart Wilderness. His heart lay here above the Chewaucan on the way to Moss Pass. He thought about the winters he and Bev had lived in that cold cabin in the desert, joyfully happy, in the years before the accident when their eyes were still filled with the stars of clear desert nights.

He walked through a large stand of old Ponderosa pines backed with sheer cliffs. There was ample room between the cliffs and the edge on the far side of the Ponderosas for any hikers to feel very comfortable, even to camp. *Here it is—I can see the whole Chewaucan Valley.* He'd mark a side trail here for those who wanted to get nearer the edge for an unobstructed view of river.

Back in the woods, he shrugged off his backpack and leaned against a Ponderosa. Unzipping his pack with his teeth, he fisted out the map to mark this, a great trail location and vista point. With his pen in his mouth, he marked the spot. Pleased, he headed downhill for a few hundred feet, Willy following close behind. He noticed his sock stayed in place between his boot and stumped right foot. When he came to the clearing, he paused, looking at the easiest way up the hill. Of course, it would be a traverse, but up ahead was the bend of a runoff ditch. He planned a small hairpin turn there before heading up the incline to Moss Pass. He stepped with the renewed vigor across the openness of the steep hillside.

The closer he got to the pass, the more he heard and felt the wind coming down. Once on top and full in the stiff blow, he braced his large frame evenly on his feet and scanned a portion of the enormous Goose Lake Valley to the east and a hundred miles beyond that, to Nevada. The ground was muddy where he stood.

I'll take them across this broad saddle. Need to tap into that spring. Could put a horse water trough in here. Yeah. I'll put the trail right above it. Then down through this aspen grove.

Beautiful! he thought.

He sat down in the aspens out of the wind, grabbed the sandwich container with his fists, peeled the lid off with his teeth, then positioned the sandwich between his clawed fists. Done, he gave the crust to Willy and, sandwich container empty, poured some water in it. Willy lapped it dry. Four cookies later, lunch was done. Containers in the pack, he grabbed the zipper between his teeth and slid it down its track.

He went back the same way to make sure the trail worked in both directions. Less than halfway down, the socks had slipped and his right foot, the one amputated to the metatarsal, nosed forward into the boot's stiff toe with every step. Try as carefully as she might, Bev could not position the stuffed socks so they stayed in place for very long, especially on a long downhill. It was a relief to sit in his pickup where the balled-up socks were now merely a nuisance and not something he'd swear at.

Chapter 2

When they first arrived in Paisley, a small town along eastern Oregon's Chewaucan River a few miles south of Summer Lake at the northwest end of the Great Basin, Larry was still in his wheelchair. He began his recovery regimen by soaking regularly in Summer Lake Hot Springs. Enclosed in an old weathered building, the large pool is still good for a slow leisurely swim from end to end or for a float and soak as the sulphur smell seeps in and relaxes muscles and mind. Larry also took daily walks through the sagebrush. His first walk was only 50 feet, but what a sense of pride he felt as he plunked down again in his wheelchair.

Across the next 20 years, the desert became as familiar to him as his own back yard. In his studies at Western Oregon College, he focused on Shakespeare and archeology. By the time of the accident he had already discovered many Lake County vision quest sites, petroglyphs, old caves, tools, and much more. He developed a solid knowledge of the geologic and human history of the area.

Larry's first trip to the desert was as an infant. A couple of years before his father left for Korea, his parents brought him on his first visit to his mother's Uncle Archie Matlock's ranch. Many trips later when Larry was eight, his widowed mother took him on yet another visit and his awareness of the archeological beauty of the High Desert began. Camping in the sagebrush along Silver Creek with Uncle Archie, the boy found a large, willow-leaf shaped piece of obsidian. Uncle Archie had walked right by it. When Larry held this perfect, beautiful black sliver of rock toward the sky, he saw milky striations through its now gray thinness. "It's a knife blade, Larry," Uncle Archie told him. "The people who lived and hunted in this desert long, long ago camped right here. His uncle had unknowingly thrown the hook to archeology. Larry thought, *Camped right here. Thousands of years ago. Wow!* He heard their footsteps, saw a few families setting up camp. He saw a boy not much older than he crouched on the side of the creek chipping and flaking this piece of obsidian he now held in his hand. This very piece! He felt its weight, heavy in time, light in substance.

Far longer ago than the knife blade, over 65 million years ago, the Cascade Mountains were new volcanic islands in the coastal Pacific. The ancient coast is now the mountainous High Desert country at the north end of the Great Basin. As the volcanic islands grew to form the high mountain range, water trapped on the eastern side formed lakes. Until about 7,000 to 9,000 years ago, when the land began to dry, the area had remained lake country. Fort Rock, the remains of an ancient volcanic cone, contained artifacts including a pair of 9,000-year-old sandals. A hundred miles farther south on the shores of the now-dry Chewaucan Lake are human remains dating from over 12,000 years ago. The flavor of southeastern Oregon is now captured in its mountains, desert, lakes, forests, and human history beginning with the archeology of the peoples of the Fort Rock and Chewaucan areas and the Modoc, Klamath, and Piute tribes. Ancient indications of these old peoples abound.

After the Civil War, the United States sent its soldiers to the West for exploration and development; some of their old military roads are still in use in Eastern Oregon. A few are paved state highway roads; others cut across vast swaths of ranch or through forests. Lake County then contained the largest Ponderosa pine forests in the Northwest. By the turn of the twentieth century, Lakeview, the county seat, boasted

10 lumber mills. Simultaneously, in the late 1800s, cattle ranching began, and Irish and Basque immigrant sheepherders arrived. In 1906, a cattleman association boasted in a letter to the Portland paper that they had killed 8,000 sheep that year, usually tying up and blindfolding the hapless owners and herders. Oregon's citizenry became enraged and the sheep and cattle wars in the state came to an immediate end. Much of this open land was soon to become national forest.

In a 1903 speech to the Society of American Foresters, Teddy Roosevelt stated that the object of his proposed Forest Service was "not to preserve forests because they are beautiful...nor because they are refuges for the wild creatures of the wilderness...; but the primary object of our forest policy, as the land policy of the United States, is the making of prosperous homes. Every other consideration comes as secondary." The agency Congress formed for this purpose was the National Forest Service. Now within the Department of Agriculture, it began in 1906. In the same year, to preserve forests because they are beautiful and to provide refuges for the creatures of the wilderness, Congress also passed the Organic Act, which began the National Parks Service, a division of the Department of Interior.

Today about a third of Lake County is national forest land with multiple uses—logging, cattle ranging, fishing, hunting, hiking, picnicking, and camping. The county and forest are imbued with the stark pragmatism of daily life whether seen from foot, combine, horseback, or pickup. Ranchers with a university degree or two in agriculture or business, loggers, and Forest Service workers live the reality and solitude of daily life tending this rural land that provides their livelihood. Life is comprised of backbreaking work accepted without question.

In May 1984, Larry got his first job in over two years. He worked part time for the City of Paisley mowing the roadsides and plowing snow. The pleasure of getting a job mixed with bad news that summer when Larry and Bev received a call from Garibaldi that Dan Fisher, the man who had cut his hand and could not go out on the fateful trip, had died. Drunk, he was killed in a one-car accident. It hit Larry hard. He knew that Dan had had a lot of problems ever since the accident. Dan figured if he had gone, the accident wouldn't have happened and Dick would still be alive. While that was probably true, it did not make Dan responsible for Dick's death, but no one could convince Dan of that. The immediate reason that Dan was off in the woods drinking by himself was an argument he'd had earlier that day with his girlfriend. For Larry, Dan's death stood as yet another fatality of the *Fargo* disaster.

That summer, Larry went to work for the local Forest Service doing something he loved—he was an archeological technician conducting cultural surveys and writing up the findings for the Forest Service and the State Historical Preservation Office. He was now doing one of those 700,000 things some doctor had told him were his remaining options.

While his mobility had returned to normal and he managed to get around the desert quite well, his feet still constantly pained him. The front of his left foot that had no toes ran into the edge of the boot on his extended walks. The two stuffed socks between the boot toe and the stubbed end of his right foot still shifted and his long walks continued to be painful and awkward. He refused to complain or be slowed, but his pain was obvious to Bev. After years of trying various orthopedic shoes and inserts, in 2003 he found a doctor in Bend, Scott Peterson, a podiatrist and the son of a cobbler. Having Larry stand on a rubber mat and seeing the computer image and pressure points of his feet, Peterson built inserts that fit into an off-the-rack extra-wide boot that worked perfectly on his Kunta Kinte amputation. To amputate only the toes, a person is still left with the balls of his feet...enough to push off for a run. To amputate behind this leaves the person without the ability to run, a technique owners sometimes used on runaway slaves, thus the name Kunta Kinte amputation. Larry labels 2003, 21 years after the accident, as the year he finally "recovered" from his injuries. *Although permanently disabled, he could now walk without constant pain.* In truth though, the constant pain continues to crop up somewhere.

Chapter 3

In January 1988, the Forest Service hired Larry fulltime. He acquired other responsibilities in addition to his work as the archeological technician and Paisley area recreation manager. He became the Fremont Forest trails program manager, recreation program liaison, writer of environmental assessments required for all timber sales contracts, and, what soon became a life mission, supervisor of building the Fremont National Recreation Trail (NRT). Shortly after the 1990 passage of the Americans with Disabilities Act (ADA), he became an active leader in Pathfinders, the Forest Service's new national group for people with disabilities.

Hiring Larry was a decision his supervisor, Roger King, would never regret. For many people a government job is just that—a job, but Roger believed that people working for the government were public servants in the truest sense of the word, people serving people. Larry, with all his previous experience working independently in the private sector, took on his responsibilities as a vocation that captured his heart and fed his soul as much as the sea had done. True of fishing, true of the Forest Service, he didn't pay attention if he worked during the week as well as the weekend. He hiked any day of the week choosing routes for future trails. He had taken over the mission of building the Fremont NRT.

As a boy exploring woods and streams and as a fisherman, Larry had always enjoyed being alone. Now he had an opportunity to explore the proposed extensive desert and forest region of the Fremont in fine detail. Part of the Fremont NRT was already complete from the California border up Lake County's highest peak of 8,347 feet, Crane Mountain, and beyond through meadows and across creeks and mountains. It was Larry's responsibility to lay out a large portion of the specific route, coordinate the funding and construction of the remaining 140 miles, and maintain all trails. When completed, this portion of the NRT will be a part of the connection of the Pacific Crest Trail to the Continental Divide Trail.

He began his surveys to determine the best location for each portion. Across the next 18 years he would hike through every area roughly five times to determine the best points of interest, water sources, vistas, and primitive campsites. He also knew he needed to keep the slopes at a reasonable level of not more than a 5- to 10-percent grade, as well as build the trail for a reasonable level of difficulty. He wrote government project funding proposals to compete with 21 other national forests, and received the funding 17 out of 18 years. With these monies, Larry hired Northwest Youth Corps workers, often from inner city neighborhoods, who worked harder than they realized they'd signed up for. For eight hours a day they swung Pulaskis, and chopped earth from the side of hills to make portions of the trail across slopes sometimes as steep as 40 degrees. They moved boulders, cut down trees up to a foot in diameter, dug up all stumps in the trail, slept and ate outdoors. During construction, Larry walked each segment of the trail anywhere from 10 to 15 times taking people in, supervising them, seeing they had supplies and a great attitude. All this meant that across these first 15 years of his Forest Service career Larry frequently walked 10 to 15 miles a day still with socks stuffed in the toes of his boot. It was awkward and painful, but the trail had come to embody his life's passion and tremendous enthusiasm for recreation and archeology.

Continuing to impress Roger, Larry insisted that the severely vandalized Bald Butte Lookout not be razed as fire practice but be restored.

"That's fine," said Roger, "but no one's going to give us the budget to save it. We're gonna burn it."

"Let me see what I can do."

"OK, I'll let you see what you can do, but unless you can come up with a plan for no budget and then how we're going to use the lookout, I'm going to have the fire crew burn it."

Once again, Larry came through on a budget of nothing. The Forest Service archeologist, John Kaiser, helped write a "Passport in Time" grant, and when approved, they supervised a volunteer crew from various parts of the country. With donated tools, time, material, and generator power, they reconstructed Bald Butte Lookout using its original materials, including renovating the doors and windows, making finely crafted reproductions only as needed. The Lakeview High School shop class of 1994 built the furniture—a table, benches, chairs, a stool, a bed frame, and a Hoosier cabinet—from original 1930s Forest Service plans. Thanks to Larry's work ethic, knowledge, and initiative, this is now one of four former Fremont Forest Service lookouts rented for $30 a night, the only rental lookout in the Pacific Northwest that is wheelchair accessible. As Roger said, "Larry could have said 'Yeah, we don't have to get it done,' and gone about his routine work." But not much about Larry is routine.

When he sent in a proposal for building 10 miles of trail and the budget returned allowed for only five, he found volunteers to make up the rest so that all 10 miles were completed within his timeline. Almost a financial story of the tortoise and the hare, the government would be happy if all its workers were so ingenious.

Chapter 4

After Congress passed the Americans with Disabilities Act (ADA) in 1990, Larry was one of the people who immediately became active in the rights, upward mobility, and employment of people with disabilities within the Forest Service. The Forest Service had had a benign civil rights department. As a result, people affected with disabilities began an organization called The Pathfinders Employee Association. In 1992 he was a part of the committee that wrote the organization's charter and was requested to go to Washington, D.C. to sign the charter. With his sense of fiscal responsibility to the Forest Service, and his supervisor being out of the office, Larry declined.

By 1993, he was a Governing Council member of Pathfinders, and soon became the editor of the association's electronic newsletter, which he wrote, published, and mailed to the Washington, D.C. office to distribute to the 5,000 Pathfinder members. The newsletter included items such as how to get a job or advancement, how to find reasonable accommodations, take an airline flight or fill out a résumé, and he always ended it with a joke. In 1995, Pathfinders elected him its vice chairperson. He went on to serve as Chairperson from 1997 to 2002.

When the Forest Service asked for volunteers to check accessibility compliance in the capital's hotels, Larry volunteered. The next thing he knew, he was on an airplane for D.C., part of a team of 10 people with disabilities to check out 20 hotels to ensure they were accessible and could be used by any government employee traveling on business. As many people do, he had often cussed the government that took place so many miles away. As he and Bev explored the city, the Washington Monument in its perfect and pure plainness brought tears to his eyes. Wherever he was, he stood stunned by the reality and beauty of Washington, D. C., its architecture, and his sense of pride and patriotism. Lincoln, accompanying his father there on a later trip movingly described their visit to the Korean War Memorial. The memorial consists of a company of soldiers, such as Larry's father might have led, crossing a rice paddy, made all the more real that day as rain pelted down on solid soldiers in their capes and gear, now literally in a field of water...statues in the rice paddy viewed by the son and grandson of a lieutenant killed in Korea.

Flown to the nation's capital again, this time to receive an award for his editorship of the Pathfinder's newsletter, he had his picture taken with the Forest Service Chief in his office. Still in use in that office was the desk of the first chief of the Forest Service, Gifford Pinchot. When the current chief left the room, Larry remained in the office long enough to sit in his chair and put his feet on the chief's desk. Bev took a picture of this sacrilege. Larry showed it to Roger King on his return to Paisley. Roger, an old-school person and government worker was appalled, "madder than hell at me," as Larry put it.

He said, "How dare you put your feet on Gifford Pinchot's desk. He's the man who began the Forest Service."

"Oh Roger. Get over it," replied Larry. "What'd you expect me to do? They left the room. I had a camera." He laughed at his opportunity and guts to commit the sacrilege. Roger, able to relate the incident as if it were his error getting upset, did get over it quickly. Larry, with his spunk and humor, could get away with about anything.

The Forest Service, based on a paramilitary model, had been an able-bodied, white male dominated organization for 90 years. The ADA changed that...and Larry was one of those leaders who helped promote its implementation. When he first arrived in Washington, D. C., he did not seem to notice that people in upper echelon positions, including the Chief, were his superiors. His life history and personal charm had served to equalize his perspective. According to one of his Washington superiors, Larry Payne, Larry Hills emerged as a well-known national leader among a field of giants, and remained a popular, well-thought-of person. Part of reason for this is his strategic vision and hard work, but it is also his dedication to the trails and serving as a motivator for these volunteers or paid workers to help him build and maintain the trails.

Those with disabilities owe Larry a great deal. Perhaps a part of this comes from the emotional truth of something Lincoln said of his father (and, like father like son, of himself). "Anything you can't do is your fault. What you do accomplish is not worth mentioning." Such an attitude tends to make a person work harder. It was not Larry Hills who told about his career accomplishments but those who had been his Forest Service supervisors and colleagues. The same traits that helped him survive entrapment on the *Fargo* help him rise above his disability and the subsequent life challenges that do not cease. He has overcome obstacles few of us ever have to face.

So successful in his work for and with those with disabilities, in addition to his 22 monetary and numerous nonmonetary awards, Larry received a promotion in 2000 to be the Forest Service EEO (Equal Employment Opportunity)/Civil Rights Program Manager as well as the Forest Recreation and Trails Coordinator for the Fremont and Winema Forests. His promotion meant Larry and Bev needed to move to Lakeview where his new office was. His supervisor was now Gary Weldon, a Vietnam veteran whose passion for 40 years has been civil rights. An EEO position is not for the faint of heart, nor does it bring much positive support and recognition. Gary said of Larry, "He's done a lot, lot, lot more than [the trail]. I believe the backbone of the Forest Service is people like Larry, people who just go on and do the work, people who have an unusually strong commitment to and love of their work." Weldon's honor came when he and Larry went to a meeting together and had to go through the buffet line. At Larry's request and need, Gary filled his plate.

In 2003 Larry decided to leave the EEO position and return to his passion and full-time work in recreation.

Abigail B. Calkin

Chapter 5

The nation has three major national recreation trails—the Appalachian, the Continental Divide, and the Pacific Crest. The latter two go from the Mexican to the Canadian borders. The Appalachian is considered the easiest of the three and the Continental Divide, due to its variable weather and altitude, the most challenging. Across the country are shorter trails, some in national parks, some on Forest Service or Bureau of Land Management (BLM) lands. It is still possible to walk across the U.S. almost continuously through these pristine areas.

Frequently used by two equestrian groups, the Fremont trail has a tread width of 18 to 24 inches and a clearing width of 8 feet, but the space and views give the feeling the trail is 10 yards or 10 miles wide. About every quarter mile, Larry has nailed NRT signs or reassurance markers to the stately Ponderosa pine trees, getting the nail out of the bucket, putting it between his teeth to insert in the sign and tree before hitting it in with the back end of his small axe head. Unforested areas have rock cairns. In addition, the trails are regularly marked with deer, cattle, horse and mule tracks. Badger, pine marten, cougar, and coyote and bear tracks and scat also mark the trails with varying frequency. In the first few weeks of fall, the mosquitoes, black flies, and searing desert heat are gone, but the snow has not yet arrived. During deer season, hunters are infrequent enough not to cause a problem for other users.

In 10 days of solo backpacking, I was pleasantly surprised to run into three ATV users, a couple day-hiking, two pairs of successful hunters, and two friends of Larry's who do chainsaw trail maintenance. I gave a silent nod or said a cheerful hello to the jets from Kingsley Air Force Base, 100 miles to the west, as they arrived each morning to overfly the desert and break the sound barrier. As I looked east to Guano Valley and Hart Mountain where the pilots overflew, my thoughts wandered to my husband's grandfather, P. P. Barry, first tending his sheep, then working his Guano Valley sheep and cattle ranch. I thought of the hardness of that life and whether the Kingsley pilots ever gave an idle thought to the people who had struggled to tame this land. Probably not.

Some summers on my morning swim in the Lakeview pool, I stared up at the two passenger jets flying over, wondered their points of origin and destination. Months after my hike, after the snows had come and gone, I flew from Seattle to San Diego. I saw Silver Lake, rectangular Summer Lake, and Abert Rim. There are the North Warners I hiked, Round Mountain, and Moss Pass! I could see the dirt roads but not the trails, recognize the mountain shapes and slopes. I stared at Rogger Meadow, Lakeview, Crane Mountain. Suddenly, there was Thomas Creek—I was flying over my sister- and brother-in-law's ranch. There's the hospital, the helipad, and two blocks up Seventh Street is my husband's and my house, recognizable by the giant poplar tree in the side yard even from 29,000 feet above or on Google Earth. Having seen them from the air, I appreciated the glories of Summer and Goose Lake Valleys and the mountains surrounding them in a way I never would have if I hadn't responded to the ad for Beverly Hills' Wallpapering in the weekly Lake County Examiner. Larry's survival of his commercial fishing accident caused me to hike this country with a different and more intimate perspective than the one my husband and I have had as we have driven and walked the countryside.

Wildlife signs included a single print of a bear cub paw and several days later, adult bear scat with its well-masticated pinecones noticeably different from that of Willamette Valley or Alaska bears. Occasional prints of the elusive cougars were fairly frequent, yet in over 20 years of working in the forest, Larry still waits to sight one. I saw one on the trail one day. He was walking straight toward me, or from his perspective, I was walking straight toward him. The sunlight gleamed off his fur as he padded down the trail, each step slightly raising a shoulder. I shouted "Hello, Cougar." He stopped. We stood staring at one another. I clapped, blew the Forest Service whistle, shouted more. He didn't move. Nor did I other than waving my arms. We stood there long enough for the sunlight to change when my cougar turned back into the hellebore he had always been. My pulse slowed and I continued my hike.

Chipmunk sightings occurred several times each day. The "wildest" large animals sighted were cows not yet taken to their lower winter ranges, startled by my presence and quick to run away. In the evenings after I set up my tent and fixed supper, I watched the sunset and enjoyed a cup of tea as the coyotes yipped. When daylight dimmed, I watched the stars emerge—the Big Dipper, Orion, Cassiopeia, Pleiades, the Milky Way's mass across the sky. I found it impossible to crawl in my tent until I had lain on the hard ground to observe the clear, expansive sky, but as the temperature dropped into the 30s, evening chill drove me from my reverie. With enough light left to stash my food 300 feet from the tent in its animal-deterrent sack, I retreated to my bivvy tent and down bag, my book and journal.

In spite of seeing someone almost each day, though, what I found was immense solitude. Too immense for me. Knowing how much solitude I normally have, I thought I'd be able to enjoy days of it on end. I had looked forward to it. I failed. It was more intense than felt comfortable, only increasing my astonishment and deep admiration for Larry's forced solitude and physical survival.

Amazing. How did he do it? I pondered. What a slouch I am out here talking to myself. Coaxing myself down into one more valley, up one more hill to find yet another rise or, even better, an astounding view that takes away my breath or brings tears to my eyes. In Alaska, I live on the edge of four contiguous national and provincial parks of the U.S. and Canada, yet I still remain awed by Lake County's wild and expansive beauty. What this timber and desert land offers is what John Muir spoke of—the salvation of mountains and wildness, the peace and solitude for "thousands of tired, nerve-shaken over-civilized people." It offers the luxury of stepping outside everyday life.

To walk the trail is to sense life's only purpose—to hear and see Clark's nutcrackers, ravens, magpies, red-tailed hawks, and falcons, to smell the scent of pine or juniper, to cross over the next hill or walk along the ridge, and to hear false hellebore rattle its long, dry autumnal brown in an afternoon wind. To hike in solitude in the twenty-first century is to glimpse part of our nation's history: What a lone person 200 years ago may have felt on first seeing this country—astounding unblemished vistas of mountain and valley, miles of country crossed and yet to cross under a blue sky that never terminates, and rare potential dangers from man or animal concurrent with profound inner peace.

Larry's distant ancestor, Cornelius Joel Hills was a cooper in northern New York who had badly injured his right foot one day on the job. Unable to work, he headed for Wisconsin to join his family, hobbling on his severely cut and almost gangrenous foot, stopping at local saloons to buy a bottle of whiskey not to drink but to douse his foot to keep away worse infection. Eventually, he continued on to Oregon. As I paused to look at the expanse of mountains and valleys between, I could picture Cornelius Hills walking alone relishing the silence and beauty of endless sky and mountains or pausing to view a herd of antelope or deer in the distance.

Larry has not lost his childhood joy of being alone in the outdoors. He still roams hills and creeks sometimes taking the axe or machete he had as a boy. It is when he is alone that this socially gracious, intelligent, and witty man feels most comfortable. Once he finished the fight, resistance, screaming and yelling about the fear and unfairness of being trapped alone at sea, and stared down death's maw, he knew that all life is preparation for that final, immanent moment. "However," he said, "The moment my brain processed the reality of what had just happened and what my situation was, I felt a sense of aloneness I never want to feel again." So it was having lost the solitude of the open ocean, he returned to the desert.

Having been through such a loss of life, further punctuated by the ultimate loneliness, Larry knew it did not matter how many times he tells himself it was not his fault, he did what he could, and came close to losing his own life, no matter how many times he reviews it in his mind in all the possible ways it could have turned out, the reality remains: Guilt and profound sorrow for Dick and what might have been took up residence in his heart and thoughts for the remainder of his days. It is perhaps this profound sorrow coupled with a small tingling pleasure of survival that motivates those who have lived through events such as this to take on an extra portion of life in an attempt to express through action what might have been.

Larry thinks about Dick almost every day. He was a good person who wanted to work and to be more than the usual waterfront guy on a dock. Straightforward, honest, and likable, Dick was going to make it whatever he decided to do. All the more reason for Larry to feel badly about his early demise on the *Fargo*. It will haunt him until the day he dies, so he tries to keep these thoughts in a portion of his mind so they don't torture him beyond sanity.

It is the law of the sea that the captain is responsible for his vessel and all souls on board whether it be one crew or 2,500 crew and passengers. How many lives had Leslie Hills been responsible for? What were his feelings when one of his men was killed? Larry has such conversations with his father while driving, hiking, falling asleep. He knows he now has a permanent identification with him: the feeling of responsibility for a life not saved. But this one person he could talk to, the most important person who could understand, is not available to exchange the few sentences that would acknowledge their shared personal grief and level, at least for the moment, the density of that feeling.

In his years as a fisherman, Larry had the motion of the water beneath the vessel. Now he walks the ancient ocean, the solid soil and rock of the mountains, alkali and desert lake beds. He has helped build trails for those whose lives are pavement and city lights so they may experience an original part of our land, enjoy the pleasures of walking on earth, of listening to birds, wind, and silence, of smelling trees, grasses, and sage, of seeing mountains and valleys, trails and blue sky with starlit nights, desert and forest flowers in bloom. He has helped build a small portion of the national trail. One hundred years from now this trail through the mountainous forest of the Oregon Outback will still offer the opportunity to shed the skin of jagged nerves and send hikers home with a peace that will last for weeks or a lifetime because Larry has helped to plant the seeds for peace of mind and strength of body.

His legacy lives in more than his survival; it lives in the leadership he has offered those with disabilities. It lives under the feet and in the thoughts, feelings, and memories of those who travel any portion of the trail. Walking up Moss Pass, I met a hunter carrying his deer a good mile to his pickup on the opening day of hunting season. He announced to me, "Tell him thank you! I appreciate this trail!"

I smile and say I shall—and I do. I ponder the resilience of the man who made this trail, admire—yes, even envy—his drive, but I also ponder the thanks this hunter doesn't know he owes to the Coast Guard and doctors who saved Larry's life, to the families—his wife's and the Forest Service people—that have offered him support. Yet it is a life always shaded by the shimmering image of the *Fargo*, when at dusk many years ago it leaded its hull to the black of the ocean floor under the weight of Susan Cooley's words.

APPENDICES

LIVES LOST

From October 1981 through March 1982, the winter commercial fishing season, at least 40 lives were lost in Oregon and Washington disasters. In tribute to them, I list their names or vessels. The information was gleaned from *The Oregonian's Northwest Magazine*. Other than Dick Cooley, I regret I was unable to learn the names of those lost after mid-January 1982.

Capt. Frank Olson, 44, USCG HH-3F helicopter pilot and Commander
   at Brookings, OR, while on a rescue mission
Phil Sutherland, 58, Puget Sound, WA
Bobby Chisum, 22, Hammond, OR
Gilbert Morrison, 21, Hammond, OR
Brian McGuire, 20, Warrenton, OR
Gary Cutting, 36, Newport, OR
Willis Easley, Coos Bay, OR
Doug Johnson, Coos Bay, OR
T. J. Foley, Coos Bay, OR
Gary Stevens, 38 Shelton, WA
Frank Welchel, Springfield, OR
Joseph Clements, Florence, OR
John Samuel, Florence, OR
Bill Dolman, home port unknown
Dave Carpenter, home port unknown
Dick Cooley, 27, Garibaldi, OR
4 gillnetters, Puget Sound, WA
3 crew from *The Shawn*
8 crew from the *F/V Midnight Express*, *F/V American Express*, and the
   F/V Corey P.
All crew from the *F/V Venezia*

The lost boats include *F/V Aloha*, *F/V American Express*, *F/V Annie B.*, *F/V Avenger*, *F/V Corey P.*, *F/V Christina J.*, *F/V Cygnet*, *F/V Debonair*, *F/V Frank*, *F/V Inez*, *F/V Mariah*, *F/V Mary Jean*, *F/V Merrimac*, *F/V Midnight Express*, *F/V Odyssey*, *F/V Oregon Otter*, *F/V Shawn*, and *F/V Venezia*.

NOTES

Part II. Trawling

p. 14. There is a significant difference between trawling and trolling that most people on land miss. A trawler has a drum or huge cylinder on the back of the vessel that turns to let out and then pull in the net that is dragging on the ocean floor. The purpose of this net is to catch all the desired fish. The major problem with trawling is that it catches everything. It is the equivalent of clear-cutting a forest; it denudes the ocean floor. It also gathers a lot of byproduct. Halibut and salmon are two fish not allowed to be caught in a trawl net; however, they get in there anyway and must be thrown away as it is not legal to benefit from bycatch. One example of a trawler often heard about are the factory trawlers.

Trolling, on the other hand, is having poles out on either side and perhaps the stern of the boat, each pole with a number of baited lines.

p. 23. Harvard psychologist Skinner saw when he rewarded pigeons according to a fixed time schedule, whatever the pigeon did just before the reward, such as turning in circles or bobbing, it repeated before the next reward. Thus, he had taught pigeons to be superstitious, to learn erroneously that if it turned or bobbed, it got a reward.

p. 25. A captain does not necessarily own the boat he operates, but he still refers to and considers it "his boat."

p. 33. Winds of 40 knots are gale force.

p. 38. The unofficial Coast Guard motto is that they have to go out, but they are not required to come back. Around the turn of the twentieth century, a crewmember about to embark on a dangerous rescue from Cape Hatteras asked, "What if we don't make it back?" Keeper Patrick H. Etheridge, of the U.S. Life Saving Service and skipper of the rescuing vessel said, "The Blue Book says we've got to go out and it doesn't say a damn thing about having to come back." The rule in the book stated that no excuse would be accepted until the Coast Guard had tried by several methods if the first way did not succeed, but the only way not to go was to try all ways until each failed. In attempting to rescue Olson and his crew, Shultz tried for an hour and was not successful.

In 1915, the U.S. Revenue Cutter System, which had been established in 1790, and the U.S. Life-Saving Service, formed in 1871, combined to form what is today's U. S. Coast Guard.

p. 40. De Becker, in *The Gift of Fear,* and Gonzales in *Deep Survival,* each have tens of examples that it is the coldly rational person who remains alert, analytical, and persistent, who survives.

Part III. The Night Orion Fell

p. 47. Larry's father, Lt. L. Bruce Hills, was with the U.S. Army's 81st Division in Anguar, Peleliu, Guadalcanal, Negarigo, New Caledonia, and Leyte before going to Japan for occupation duty. He returned to the States in August 1946, married, had a son in 1947, and was called back to active duty in 1950 to go to Korea.

p. 57. Lt. Dave Glenn was one of five officers who shared this position. The two others did not remember the case and, therefore, assumed they were not involved. No one was able to locate the other two who had resigned from the Coast Guard before retirement. Glenn does not recall which shift he served, but he knew the details of the accident and rescue as if he had been on duty both Wednesday and Thursday. Since he initially thought he had done the plan, he told me the events as if he had been the person doing the initial CASP. If he had not done the CASP, then he would have read that plan very carefully to assist in finishing the SAR on Thursday. For the sake of names and details, I used his version assuming he had probably done the initial SAR plan. I apologize if it was another officer who did the original plan.

In 1982, such plans took about three hours. These days the SAR plans are complete within about 20 minutes thanks to GPS systems and advanced computer technology.

p. 64. Thanks to Greg Streveler, Gustavus, Alaska, for his analysis of the seas in the North Pacific.

p. 83. People have questioned how Larry could have four wraps of hose line, steel cable, on his arms yet the line did not wrap around his torso. I bought a Bendy doll, tied a fishing line to her wrist and rapidly and briefly wound the crank handle, fast enough that I could not perceive the details of what was happening to the doll and the line. When I stopped the reel, I was surprised to see each arm of the doll had four wraps of fishing line. None was across her torso and one was behind her neck. Thus, when Larry ducked his head, he did indeed probably save his own life. For me as the writer, any misunderstanding or doubts that I may have had regarding Larry's position and the number of wraps evaporated.

p. 89. "Highwayman," Johnny Cash, 1965. This song is also on the Waylon Jennings, Willie Nelson, Johnny Cash, Kris Kristofferson 1985 CD *Highwayman*, Columbia Records, with Nelson singing the last verse, the one that kept repeating in Larry's thoughts.

Part IV. Semper Paratus

p. 115. Much of the information about what happened on deck initially came from listening to David tell his recollections of the accident and rescue to Larry and me. Twenty-two years after the fact, these two men had just discussed for the first time the most tragic moment in their relationship. David, not a man with great variation in facial expression or voice tone, took a long look at Larry. Sadness seeped into him until the natural contours and lines of his face deepened and he aged 10 years in that moment of compassion for his brother-in-law.

Much of the information also came from the Coast Guard. In the end, I had 10 different versions of what happened at the Coast Guard stations in Garibaldi, in Astoria, and on board the *Fargo* and in the helicopters. Most of the differences were just missing pieces, but some were outright contradictions. This was one reason to send the rescue portions of the book—from David Vandecoevering's first phone call to the 1489 crew en route to Tillamook—to those involved in the rescue.

The corrections and educated opinions have been invaluable.

p. 115. Finding the Coast Guard involved in this rescue took three years; two people I never found. I first found John Whiddon through the Pterodactyl site, the Coast Guard officers' website. He led me to RADM Dave Kunkel, who turned out not to be on the rescue but a critical person in locating other officers.

I found George MacGillis through a web search. Portland, Maine, or Portland, Oregon? I'll try Oregon first because that's where Garibaldi is.

"Were you in the Coast Guard in 1982?"

"1982, yeah, but I'm very bad with names."

"It was out of Astoria station and the boat was from Garibaldi. A commercial fishing disaster."

"The *Fargo*. Yah, I remember that. I have PTSD partly because of this. That was the first one. There were a couple other really bad ones."

"Did he save his arms?" MacGillis immediately continued. What concern he shows for this man he helped rescue, the only one who asked such a direct question.

I heard Ray Shultz worked for a life star helo company out of Portland. I called. He no longer worked there. Only one pilot knew him, but hadn't spoken to him for a year. He called him. Shultz called me. We talked many times. He checked his logbook and found that Gary Ellis was his co-pilot. Ellis chose not to respond to me, but I continued to send him sections of the book that involved him in the hope that if I had made some grievous error that he would reply with a correction.

The process involved the initial contact by phone. The contacts grew to e-mail exchanges and more phone calls. MacGillis prodded me yet again one more time to find Lutz. When I finally found Lutz, he had saved all the reports from the case—including photographs, Ellis' log, the ops reports, and letters of appreciation. He was leaving on another month-long FEMA job soon, and we spent 15 hours of the next two days talking and e-mailing. "Shouldn't you be spending this time with your family?" I asked. "If you've been looking for me for three years, I'm not going to make you wait another month," he replied. Once again, I thought what are these Coasties (and former Coasties) made of? Iron?

As I continued to write about them and what they'd done, it became obvious that I needed to meet these people face to face. The background information was very helpful when I finally sat down with each one. I could concentrate on their faces and body language as well as hear their words. Hardly a conversation occurred without deep emotions coming to the surface, often with tears about this rescue or another. Passion lies within the soul of each of these Coasties…enough to melt their hearts into compassion for the men they rescue.

p. 115. The first level involved in a rescue is the local station (Tillamook Bay Station). If the situation needs greater assistance, the next level is the group station (Station Astoria), then the regional (13th Regional Command Center in Seattle), and finally, the command center (PAC, or Pacific Air Command in Sacramento). This rescue required all four of these.

p. 122. Tunnel vision is a colloquial term for "inattentional blindness," which is a psychological term for a person being so focused on a task that he does not see the elements unimportant to the immediacy of the scene or situation at hand. By necessity, it is a part of Coast Guard, or any military training.

Perhaps the best known study of "inattentional blindness" is Harvard University's study by Simons and Chabris. They looked at what people see when watching a pick-up basketball game. A person with an umbrella or in a gorilla suit walked between the players and half the viewers did not see these interruptions. It is essential that a Coast Guardsman focus on his or her task to the exclusion of irrelevant details. The result of this highly concentrated attention is that other stimuli not essential to the situation are not seen.

p. 122. John Lutz was an AT3 when he resigned. I had looked for him for over three years until that last time MacGillis once again insisted I keep on trying. On at least my sixth detailed web search, I finally located him. Having been told by an officer that he may receive more than a commendation for his part in the rescue and, therefore, he should retain all paperwork, this enlisted man was the person who had all the detailed USCG information I'd been looking for. In the last two days before he left on a month-long assignment, he spent 15 hours looking for the information, then scanning, e-mailing, faxing the items, and discussing the incident with me on the phone. He sent his drawing, written description of the rescue from his perspective both turned into his superiors within days of the rescue, his Letter of Appreciation from Capt. Ciancaglini, the report from the Ops center at Astoria—a moment by moment description of events as reported to the Seattle RCC and other local Oregon and Washington stations, co-pilot Gary Ellis' report of actions within the helo by time, latitude and longitude during the search, and the times and events once at the scene. Through these valuable reports and letters and the information from interviewing the dozen Coast Guardsmen and two fishermen involved, I pieced together the events of the search and rescue. Larry Hills, David Vandecoevering, Ray Shultz, John Whiddon, George MacGillis, and John Lutz read these parts and offered their technical and factual corrections.

p. 123. There was some conflict about how many wraps of cable Larry had over his arms. Larry insisted it was four because he counted them many times. On being told what they reported, Larry's response was "I counted four—many times I counted four wraps." Several rescuers said it was three. Larry's arms still show four scars from the cables. It is possible, however, that when the reel went backward, not only did he change position, but he may have lost one of the four wraps. It is also possible that the Coasties, dealing with the intensity of the moment and their specific roles in the rescue, did not focus on Larry's details but on rescuing him.

p. 123. The Coast Guard had a volunteer rescue swimmer program, SARWET, Sea Air Rotary Wing Evacuation Team from 1972 to 1976. The official USCG rescue swimmer program did not begin until 1985.

Rescue swimmers, then or now, were not normally lowered to the deck of a boat, especially when there is no assist from someone on the vessel.

p. 130. The name of the corpsman is not known. In his log book the pilot records the names of officers on board, the length and type of the sortie, and in the case of a hoist the number of people hoisted. He records the names of enlisted personnel and gives that manifest to ground crew.

p. 134. This was Whiddon's description 23 years later, cold off his memory. The recollection he lived with for over 20 years since the accident was the same one Larry had lived with, that Larry's and Dick's heads were 6 to 8 inches apart.

p. 139. The crew of the 44304 who stationed at Garibaldi were FN Wilburn, SA Teza, BM2 Terrell, MK1 Johnson, BM3 Culnane, and MK3 Stanford.

p. 149. Dick's lifelong and closest friend, Mickey Orr, who had also crewed with Larry on *FV Ike*, and for David, and who was to be best man at David's wedding, died from a drug overdose two month after Dick's funeral. Rodney Hamann was Fred Hamann's brother. Dan Fisher was the person who was supposed to be the third crewmember on the *Fargo*. He died two years later in a single-car accident while driving alone.

p. 170. Post-traumatic stress disorder is the current term, first used in 1980. However, an Egyptian medical source identified it around 1900 B.C.E. Certainly it is apparent in Homer's *Iliad*, Shakespeare's *Macbeth*, and on up to the U.S. Civil War when it was named Soldier's Heart, World War I's Shell Shock, and World War II's Combat Fatigue. The current term, Post-Traumatic Stress Disorder, applies to some who served in Vietnam, Iraq, and Afghanistan wars and has broadened to the civilian population who have suffered from various forms of abuse.

V. Mending

p. 183. On November 20, 2009, Susan Cooley Hadley wrote "forgive me if i curse the fargo to bottom of the sea." (http://www.scrollinspace. com under the comments section of Against the Net.)

VI. On the Trail

p. 190. Western Oregon College was called Oregon College of Education when Larry attended.

p. 192. In 1904, raiders from the cattle herders came into the tent of P. P. Barry, a recent immigrant from County Cork, Ireland. They tied him up, threatened him with death if he told, and then killed his 1800 sheep. Outlasting the sheep and cattle wars, he eventually owned a Lake County ranch and ran both animals in his herd of thousands.

p. 195. Technically known as the Southern Oregon Intertie National Recreation Trail #160 and #161, the Fremont NRT is one of many national recreation trails across the country. The best known of these are the Appalachian, the Continental Divide, and the Pacific Crest Trails.

p. 195. The Paisley Forest Service complex is a town centerpiece with its historic CCC[1] white one-story buildings trimmed and roofed in green. As other area offices modernized their furnishings from oak to metal, Roger King, the District Ranger, saw to it that the Paisley office refurbished theirs with the castoff oak period pieces. Within 10 years, the interiors of the buildings had barrister bookcases with glass fronts, oak file cabinets, desks, and chairs in keeping with the history of the town where homes were often 100 years old and ranches had been in families at least that long.

p. 195. NRT is the acronym for the National Recreation Trail. Constructed as one of the National Forest Service trails, this is a part of a trail system that extends across the country. From October 2005 to August 2006, Buckwheat Donahue walked from Florida to his home in Skagway, Alaska, on NRTs, except for a few short stints along rural highways, his passage through Canada, a three-block drive, and a couple of thousand miles by kayak and canoe. His purpose was to improve his health and raise money for the health clinic in Skagway.

p. 197. John Kaiser was the Forest Service archeologist who assisted on this project.

p. 198. Chuck Graham was Larry's supervisor when Larry had his first opportunity to go to the national Pathfinders meeting in Washington, D. C., to sign the organization's charter. With his sense of fiscal responsibility to the Forest Service and Chuck being out of the office, Larry declined. While Chuck appreciated Larry's fiscal responsibility, he was not happy, and pointed out Larry's contribution to the Forest Service and to the leadership of those with disabilities was of much greater value than the cost.

GLOSSARY

Bell—the attachment at the open end of the smallest part of the trawl net where the fish are forced by the direction of the boat and force of the water. Usually made of brass, it closes the cod end during trawling.

Belly—Located between the cod end and the square opening, the belly of the net holds the fish once the cod end is full.

Bight—the middle of a slack line, or a loop or curve in the line that when tightened quickly or unexpectedly can cinch a person and can cause serious injury or death

Bowline—pronounced with a long /o/ and a short /i/; a type of common seaman's knot

Cable—also called ground gear or hose line

CASP—Computer-Assisted Search Plan

Checkers—A deck checker is a very large box with sides at least a foot high that is used to sort fish.

Chromoscope—an instrument that shows images in color; in this case it shows the changes in the ocean or ocean floor as well as the schools of fish as the vessel moves

Coastie—nickname given to the Coast Guard by Guard members

Cod end—the closed and narrow end of the net where the fish collect during a trawl

Dead man's stick—also called "dead man valve" or "spring valve," which, when released automatically, stops the drum from turning

Deckhand—person who performs any manual tasks on a vessel

Doors—attached to the net wings and ground lines these large water foils use the generated water resistance to spread the wings of the net. The *Fargo's* were 5- by 8, made of steel and weighed 1,000 pounds.

Drum—a large steel cylinder, anywhere from 6 to 12 feet long on smaller boats, used to haul and wrap the net around when bringing it in, storing it, or before releasing it to the ocean bottom

Ebb tide—low tide. To cross the Garibaldi Bar on an ebb tide is extremely dangerous. In 2004, 11 lives were lost when a charter boat crossed on an ebb tide.

Fathom—a mariner's measure of 6 feet. It comes from the length of a man's outstretched arms. The rope indicating fathoms originally had a knot tied every 6 feet and aided in measuring the depth of the water.

FV—fishing vessel

Flood tide—high tide

Flotsam—the floating wreckage of a boat or ship found in the ocean or awash on the shore

Flying bridge—the small open deck enclosed by a low gunwale, located above the pilothouse and from which the ship can be steered. On some vessels it's fully enclosed.

Gale—winds of 34 to 47 knots

Gallows posts—the fixed frame from which the doors are hung when not in use

Glow plugs—the heating element within the cylinders to start a cold diesel engine

Ground lines—Ground lines run from the doors to the lower tips of the wings in order to create a mud cloud that herds the fish into the net. They are steel cables encased in steel-embedded hose. They wrap around the drum prior to the net.

Gunwale—the top part of the side of the boat above the deck. Sometimes spelled gunnels

Helo—short for a Coast Guard helicopter

Knot—a vessel's speed in nautical miles. A nautical mile equals 6,082 feet, or the distance of one minute of arc in latitude

Lazarette—a small hold in the stern for storage

LORAN—Long Range Navigation system provides a low frequency transmission for locating specific places. The GPS and a global navigation satellite system

Net parts—cod end, belly, mouth, wings

Pigtail—the description Capt. Glenn used to describe the Fargo's path as it moved across the ocean in concentric circles

Plugged—fisherman's lingo for a hold full of fish

Pulaski—a tool with an axe head on one end and an adze on the other

RADM—Rear Admiral

Rime ice—a thin sheet of ice that freezes to a surface due to wind or rain

VHF—Very High Frequency. Boat radios have a VHF frequency. Channel 16 is the channel everyone listens to unless asked to switch to another one.

SAR—a Coast Guard <u>S</u>earch <u>a</u>nd <u>R</u>escue mission; pronounced as one word

Scootin'-'long-the-shore—a cheap, quick, hot dish of onions, potatoes, and eggs, maybe with a few slices of bacon thrown on top. Good for when the fish are coming in, or when there's little money to buy supplies for the boat.

Stokes litter—a stretcher with raised sides to move an injured person from boat, ship, ground or water to safety

Storm—Winds of 47 to 93 knot winds

Stabilizer poles—poles that extend from the sides of the boat, designed to help the boat's stability during bad weather

Shrimping—jargon indicating the boat is fishing for shrimp; requiring gear different from fish trawling

Trawling—Bottom trawling is also called dragging, where a boat pulls a net along the floor of the ocean to scoop all fish into it. It is different from trolling, seining, or gillnetting.

Wings—Called wings because they spread wide opening of the net, they lie between the belly and the ground lines. They are attached to the 5 by 8 feet, 1,000-pound steel doors.

Wheelhouse—the enclosed, secure location from which the boat is steered. The compass-mounted binnacle, navigational charts, VHF radio, and LORAN (in the days of LORAN) are all there. It is also called the pilothouse.

REPORT ON FILE AT USCG HEADQUARTERS

U.S. Coast Guard Historian's Office report of the missing *F/V Fargo*
USCG internal statement from The Department of Transportation, Coast Guard Daily Operations Highlights, Flag Plot (G-OFP/74). Date issued: 17 February 1982.

CCGD13: *F/V FARGO* (US)—OVERDUE—OREGON

Wednesday morning this 46 foot [sic] shrimper, with two persons on board was reported overdue on a fishing trip from Tillamook Bay to an area 25 miles off the entrance to the Columbia River. Two HH3 helicopters from Coast Guard Air Station ASTORIA searched Wednesday with negative results. The search was continued Thursday with two C130 aircraft from Air Station SACRAMENTO being added to the search. Thursday afternoon one of the helicopters sighted the vessel approximately 60 miles SW of Astoria. The two crewmembers were sighted on deck entangled in nets and rigging. When the helicopter lowered a crewman to the vessel it was learned that only one of the crewmembers was alive. The survivor was hoisted aboard the helicopter and transported to Tillamook County Hospital for treatment. A utility boat from Coast Guard Station TILLAMOOK BAY towed the vessel with the deceased crewmember into Tillamook Bay [sic], where it was turned over to authorities. CASE CLOSED.

The USCG Historian's Office, courtesy of Chris Halvern, provided the above statement from the Coast Guard archival files.

SITREP or OPERATIONS CENTER REPORT

OPS center (com. center?)

```
HHHHSSC
SS DE 30
ISN-SB/69
T-P TB GH CD DD
TB GH CD T STA'S
DD T MSO
P 120325Z FEB 82
FR CONCOGARDGRU ASTORIA OR
TO SEATTLESARCOORD SEATTLE WA
INFO COGARD STA TILLAMOOK BAY OR
-COGARD STA GRAYS HARBOR WESTPORT WA
COGARD STA CAPE DISAPPOINTMENT WA
COGARD MSO PORTLAND OR
COGARD MSO ASTORIA OR
BT
UNCLAS //N16133//
SUBJ: ALERT SITREP SIX, F/V FARGO LOCATED, UCN 0045
1. SITUATION:
    A. 1220U F/V FARGO LOCATED BY C-130 CGNR 1502, HH3F CGNR 1483 DIVERTED
FROM SEARCH TO SCENE. POSN 45-30N 124-13W.
    B. O/S WX: SKY BKN TO OVC, VIS 1/8 MI IN RAIN SHOWERS, SWELLS 270/15 FT,
SEAS 210/13 FT
2. ACTION:
    A. 1232U CGNR 1483 O/S, HOISTED AT3 LUTZ BY SLING ONTO APPROX 2FT X 4 FT AREA
ON F/V, EXTREMELY DIFFICULT HOIST DUE TO DECK CABLES. CGNR 1483 REPORTS ONE
PERSON ALIVE, BUT HAS BOTH ARMS CAUGHT IN NET ON WINCH. SECOND PERSON IS WRAPPED
IN NET ON NET REEL, CONDITION UNKNOWN. AT3 LUTZ FOUND HACKSAW AND ATTEMPTED TO
FREE FIRST PERSON
    B. 1249U HH3F CGNR 1489 LT WHIDDON A/B WITH DR BARNES ABOARD, ENROUTE
TILLAMOOK BAY TO PICK-UP TWO CIVILIANS FAMILIAR WITH THE VSLS WINCHES.
    C. 1316U CGNR 1489 O/D TILLAMOOK BAY
    D. 1318U CGNR 1489 A/B WITH TWO CIVILIANS IDENTIFIED AS DAVE VANDERCOUVERING
AND FRED HAMMAN OF GARIBALDI OREGON
    E. 1321U CGNR 1483 REPORTS AM2 MACGILLIS HOISTED ONTO F/V TO ASSIST AT3 LUTZ
CGNR 1483 ADVISED THE WX DETERIORATING, WINDS 15 KTS, SEAS 6-8 FT
    F. 1336U CGNR 1483 DEPARTED SCENE. ENROUTE ASTORIA
    G. 1349U CGNR 1489 O/S, HOISTED BOTH CIVILIANS ONTO F/V FARGO
    H. 1400U MLB 44309 O/S STANDING BY
    I. 1408U CGNR 1489 REPORTS ONE MAN FREE, ALIVE BUT DELERIOUS
    J. 1418U CGNR 1489 REPORTS SURVIVOR HOISTED ABOARD, DR EVALUATING.
SECOND PERSON REPORTED DECEASED
    K. 1421U CGNR 1489 DPTD SCENE WITH INJURED PERSON, ENROUTE TILLAMOOK COUNTY
GENERAL HOSPITAL. CGNR 1502 DPTD SCENE
    L. 1431U CGNR 1489 O/D TILLAMOOK COUNTY GENERAL HOSPITAL, DEPLANED SURVIVOR
TO AWAITING HOSPITAL PERSONNEL. CONDITION: TEMP 90 DEG, BLOOD PRESSURE 80, BOTH
ARMS APPEAR BROKEN, STABLE, BUT INCOHERENT
    M. 1434U DHCS ROBINSON RPTD NOW NOTIFIED
    N. 1500U CGNR 1489 A/B TILLAMOOK COUNTY GENERAL HOSPITAL, ENROUTE ASTORIA
```

ACKNOWLEDGMENTS

I would like to thank Larry, Bev, and Lincoln Hills for letting a stranger into their lives and then being so open when sharing facts, thoughts and feelings with me. My relationship with Larry and Bev has grown into a friendship. I enjoy their company and admire their many accomplishments. I'd also like to thank other family members—David Vandecoevering for his time, sharing, and openness; Marge Jordan, their sister, and her husband, Dave Jordan who rescued two others from the sinking of the *Fargo*. Two other sisters, Theresa and Mary contributed and Linda offered beautiful distractions by sending me photos of unusual events such as albino moose, quasars, and constellations. Thank you to Tony Vandecoevering for his support. The mother of this accomplished and energetic brood, Lorraine Vandecoevering has always maintained an open door for so many. I thank her for cups of tea, bowls of soup, long conversations, and details of where the VHF was, who sat or stood where, the few changes she's made to the house, and conversations about the moments of that week. My heartfelt thanks to Bev for blurting out the story in a staccato style in just a few minutes that one morning in May 2003 as she wallpapered a room in my husband's and my home in Lakeview, Oregon.

With deepest respect, gratitude, and sympathy, I would like to thank Will Cooley and Joey Anderson, the sons of Dick Cooley (Joey is technically his stepson), for walking into my life in August 2009. I had been looking for you for over six years.

Family tragedy is handed down as boldly as eye color or height. I extend my sympathies to these three young men—Lincoln, Joey, and Will. Your lives have not been smooth.

I remain deeply touched by the level of trust Larry and his family and the Coast Guard members, who were at Station Astoria in 1982, placed in me. I did not consider it when I embarked on this project, but one day I realized all of the incredibly personal information the family and the Coast Guard entrusted me with: often, glimpses into their souls —information to hold and feel honored by. I respect the privacy and integrity of it. Family members and rescuers had the opportunity to read what I said about them before it became print. Larry, Bev, and Lincoln Hills, David Vandecoevering, Ray Shultz, John Whiddon, George MacGillis, John Lutz, and Mike Wood read these parts and offered their technical and factual corrections. Thank you for your time and advice.

Living in Alaska, I knew the value of the Coast Guard before I embarked on this book. Now it is an honor to have spoken with so many of you, and to have met some of your ranks. Your openness has been not only informative but also highly refreshing. Every one of you has been honest and kind to me, a stranger who called you out of the blue. I list you by name, almost in the order in which I found you.

Scott Price and Chris Halvern, historians at Coast Guard Headquarters directed me to the retired officers site, Pterodactyl, to Fred's Place, and gave me other helpful information. Chris Halvern found and sent me the *Fargo* rescue report on file at Headquarters.

Capt. Bob Watterson, USCG, ret., for leading me to John Whiddon.

Cmdr. John Whiddon, USCG, ret., for his words, friendliness, and the amount of time he and his wife, Lauri, gave me. He also led me to RADM Kunkel.

When I first corresponded with RADM Dave Kunkel, he was at USCG Headquarters in charge of Operations, and afterward, the Regional Commander of the 7th District, Florida and the Caribbean before his retirement. He provided me with information about how the USCG functions, answered technical questions, and helped me find many people involved in the rescue.

Mark Hohstedt, a helicopter rescue pilot in the private sector had worked with Ray Shultz, and gave me his location. He gave Shultz my phone number and e-mail address.

Lt. Cmdr. Ray Shultz, USCG, ret., for his wit and dry humor, keenness of thought and memory, his way with words, his precision, and directness. He looked in his logbook and called me back within minutes stating his hours in flight on the Wednesday and Thursday SARs. He also stated Gary Ellis was his co-pilot on both flights.

Capt. Mike Moore, Operations, Headquarters USCG remembered the incident clearly. He checked his log book and gave me the durations of the SAR flights for the helo Whiddon and he flew. I appreciate his phone calls and e-mails.

George MacGillis, AM, USCG, ret., led me to Mike Moore, by remembering his name. Dave Kunkel put me in touch with Moore. George had an excellent memory of the incident. He kept trying to help me find John Lutz and, when I had given up, he insisted I try again.

John Lutz, an AT3 when he resigned, eluded me for over three years, until that last time MacGillis once again insisted I keep trying. On about my sixth web search, I finally located him. He was about to leave on a month's FEMA assignment. I reached him Thursday evening when he arrived home from work. Across the next two and a half days, we spent 15 hours communicating by e-mail, phone, and fax. He spent additional time looking for his materials on the incident. I told him to spend this time with his family. He said if I'd been waiting to find him for over three years, he wasn't going to make me wait another month for the information. My thanks to his family for the time he spent searching for the materials and communicating with me. A rich source, he, like his fellow Coasties, had an excellent memory, and in addition the gold mine I'd been hoping for—copies of all the official reports from the incident.

Capt. Dave Glenn was one of the people involved in developing the search plan at the 13th Regional Command Center in Seattle. Not only did he provide me with details of weather and ocean conditions, and vital details of this SAR, he also gave me a tour of the Regional Command Center in Juneau in 2005 when he was stationed there. While in the room where they currently develop the SAR plans, in a more sophisticated and timely manner, he took care to explain the differences between the 1982 and the 2005 procedures and plans.

RADM Dave Ciancaglini, USCG, ret. provided me with some information about Station Astoria during the early 1980s when he was the commander there. It was his excellent leadership that made Astoria the tight and supportive station it was.

Ray Shultz put me in touch with some of the Ground Crew at Station Astoria.

Mike Wood was another key person who saved Larry's life by knowing immediately this was an emergency. Wood made the call that put this case at the SAR level within minutes after David Vandecoevering called it in. Any delay of even a half a day, and there would have been two dead men in the net on the *Fargo*. He recollected the call from David Vandecoevering and told me his reasons for immediately bumping it to SAR status.

Master Chief Ron Turner, USCG, ret., was in charge of personnel, and Phil Snodgrass, E-8, Chief Petty Officer, ret., offered helpful information about Station Astoria and its crew during the early 1980s.

One 2005 day, I called Station Tillamook Bay in Garibaldi and had the good fortune to have Jim Bankson, Master Chief's Boson's Mate and CO at Tillamook Bay USCG Station in Tillamook answer the phone during the lunch hour. As it turned out, Bankson was stationed at Astoria on board the 55-foot rescue boat, *Triumph*, at the time of the accident. He gave details, including being on the *Triumph* when it tied in tandem to assist the 44 in the crossing of the Columbia River bar.

The families of these men and women from the 44 must have joined with the others at the Tillamook Bay USCG Station to fill the Hills family freezer while Larry remained in Good Samaritan Hospital in Portland. Their generosity made Bev weep not only when she found the food, but also when she told me 21 years later of their generosity.

Mike Leavitt, Master Chief's Boson's Mate and CO at Tillamook Bay USCG Station in Garibaldi in 2008, who gave me access to the situation reports, photographs, and another newspaper report in the station's scrapbook.

Lt. j.g. Adam Davenport gave me a tour of Air Station Astoria in 2008, the station where Ciancaglini, Shultz, Whiddon, Kunkel, Ellis, Moore, Lutz, MacGillis, Wood, Turner, and Snodgrass, in addition to many others, were stationed in February 1982. MKtech2 Bryan Barbuchano at Cape Disappointment in Ilwaco, WA, gave me a tour of the *Triumph*, the boat Bankson was on when it assisted in towing the *Fargo* across the Columbia River Bar. Although almost 100 miles apart, Warrenton, Ilwaco, Tillamook Bay Stations, and Astoria are all parts of Station Astoria.

John Whiddon arranged for me to tour the helicopter and C-130 section of USCG Air Station Kodiak. Lt. Steve Bond gave me a tour of the relevant aircraft. Lt. Lance Kerr and Ensign Bernie Garrigan answered some of the questions I asked as we walked through the hangars.

Four other former Coasties have been very helpful. Keith Richards had worked on a 44 when in the service. He explained to me what would have happened when the 44 towed the *Fargo*.

Wayne Clark, an ASM2, who left the USCG, was a rescue swimmer in the SARWET (Sea Air Rotary Wing Evacuation Team) days of the early 1970s when the rescue swimmers volunteered for that duty. He gave me information and read the rescue chapter and offered technical corrections.

Tom Berner, 3rd Petty Officer, another former USCG member, called me regularly, sometimes daily, to make sure I was working and to check on my progress.

I thank the Coast Guard members I visited for their openness and hospitality, including the delicious and graceful dinners Lauri Whiddon, Peg Wood, and Linda Lutz cooked and served.

Coasties, I like your intelligence, humor, wit, and openness. Thank you for rescuing Larry. Thank you for giving me the opportunity to write this book and the offer of information to make it more accurate.

had an excellent memory of the incident. He kept trying to help me find John Lutz and, when I had given up, he insisted I try again.

John Lutz, an AT3 when he resigned, eluded me for over three years, until that last time MacGillis once again insisted I keep trying. On about my sixth web search, I finally located him. He was about to leave on a month's FEMA assignment. I reached him Thursday evening when he arrived home from work. Across the next two and a half days, we spent 15 hours communicating by e-mail, phone, and fax. He spent additional time looking for his materials on the incident. I told him to spend this time with his family. He said if I'd been waiting to find him for over three years, he wasn't going to make me wait another month for the information. My thanks to his family for the time he spent searching for the materials and communicating with me. A rich source, he, like his fellow Coasties, had an excellent memory, and in addition the gold mine I'd been hoping for—copies of all the official reports from the incident.

Capt. Dave Glenn was one of the people involved in developing the search plan at the 13th Regional Command Center in Seattle. Not only did he provide me with details of weather and ocean conditions, and vital details of this SAR, he also gave me a tour of the Regional Command Center in Juneau in 2005 when he was stationed there. While in the room where they currently develop the SAR plans, in a more sophisticated and timely manner, he took care to explain the differences between the 1982 and the 2005 procedures and plans.

RADM Dave Ciancaglini, USCG, ret. provided me with some information about Station Astoria during the early 1980s when he was the commander there. It was his excellent leadership that made Astoria the tight and supportive station it was.

Ray Shultz put me in touch with some of the Ground Crew at Station Astoria.

Mike Wood was another key person who saved Larry's life by knowing immediately this was an emergency. Wood made the call that put this case at the SAR level within minutes after David Vandecoevering called it in. Any delay of even a half a day, and there would have been two dead men in the net on the *Fargo*. He recollected the call from David Vandecoevering and told me his reasons for immediately bumping it to SAR status.

Master Chief Ron Turner, USCG, ret., was in charge of personnel, and Phil Snodgrass, E-8, Chief Petty Officer, ret., offered helpful information about Station Astoria and its crew during the early 1980s.

One 2005 day, I called Station Tillamook Bay in Garibaldi and had the good fortune to have Jim Bankson, Master Chief's Boson's Mate and CO at Tillamook Bay USCG Station in Tillamook answer the phone during the lunch hour. As it turned out, Bankson was stationed at Astoria on board the 55-foot rescue boat, *Triumph*, at the time of the accident. He gave details, including being on the *Triumph* when it tied in tandem to assist the 44 in the crossing of the Columbia River bar.

The families of these men and women from the 44 must have joined with the others at the Tillamook Bay USCG Station to fill the Hills family freezer while Larry remained in Good Samaritan Hospital in Portland. Their generosity made Bev weep not only when she found the food, but also when she told me 21 years later of their generosity.

Mike Leavitt, Master Chief's Boson's Mate and CO at Tillamook Bay USCG Station in Garibaldi in 2008, who gave me access to the situation reports, photographs, and another newspaper report in the station's scrapbook.

Lt. j.g. Adam Davenport gave me a tour of Air Station Astoria in 2008, the station where Ciancaglini, Shultz, Whiddon, Kunkel, Ellis, Moore, Lutz, MacGillis, Wood, Turner, and Snodgrass, in addition to many others, were stationed in February 1982. MKtech2 Bryan Barbuchano at Cape Disappointment in Ilwaco, WA, gave me a tour of the *Triumph*, the boat Bankson was on when it assisted in towing the *Fargo* across the Columbia River Bar. Although almost 100 miles apart, Warrenton, Ilwaco, Tillamook Bay Stations, and Astoria are all parts of Station Astoria.

John Whiddon arranged for me to tour the helicopter and C-130 section of USCG Air Station Kodiak. Lt. Steve Bond gave me a tour of the relevant aircraft. Lt. Lance Kerr and Ensign Bernie Garrigan answered some of the questions I asked as we walked through the hangars.

Four other former Coasties have been very helpful. Keith Richards had worked on a 44 when in the service. He explained to me what would have happened when the 44 towed the *Fargo*.

Wayne Clark, an ASM2, who left the USCG, was a rescue swimmer in the SARWET (Sea Air Rotary Wing Evacuation Team) days of the early 1970s when the rescue swimmers volunteered for that duty. He gave me information and read the rescue chapter and offered technical corrections.

Tom Berner, 3rd Petty Officer, another former USCG member, called me regularly, sometimes daily, to make sure I was working and to check on my progress.

I thank the Coast Guard members I visited for their openness and hospitality, including the delicious and graceful dinners Lauri Whiddon, Peg Wood, and Linda Lutz cooked and served.

Coasties, I like your intelligence, humor, wit, and openness. Thank you for rescuing Larry. Thank you for giving me the opportunity to write this book and the offer of information to make it more accurate. You were all very forthcoming.

Fred Hamann, a commercial fisherman, also gave information about the rescue from the perspective of being one of those on the *Fargo* during the rescue. Small details matter. He was the one who noted that Dick Cooley's glove was snagged on the line.

Many doctors treated Larry. I thank Kathleen Langtry, Sharron Fuchs, and Keith Tichenor of the law office of Tichenor, Dziuba, & Coletti for providing me with the two boxes of hospital records, the space to go through them, and the use of their copy machine. My thanks to attorney Dan O'Leary for his role in all this.

Lyle Mohr, M.D. provided me all of the information on Larry's entry and brief stay at Tillamook General Hospital. Norman Estin, one of the 18 treating doctors in Portland's Good Samaritan Hospital read the medical chapter. Friends Colleen Stansbury, RNPA, and Victoria Bennett, RNNP, and Rob Giese, RN, answered my many medical questions with excellent explanations. My friend, Susan Farmer, M.D., also read and commented on the medical chapter.

People in the Forest Service were equally helpful. I thank Roger King, Gary Weldon, Larry Payne, Rod Stewart, and Chuck Graham for their information regarding Larry's work in the Forest Service and his role in Pathfinders.

Veronica (Ronnie) Clarno, a high school friend of Dick's, for her memories and insights into Dick.

Dave Jordan and Pete King for their information on the sinking of the *Fargo*.

Phil Fisher for his information on his brother, Dan Fisher.

The members of Gustavus Writers' Group and Topeka, Kansas writers group, Table for Eight, have offered excellent comments and suggestions, especially Eileen Clark and Laura Morris who spent many hours reading and editing.

Dawn Marano was a most insightful editor of an early draft.

Marcia Malott continues to remain my invaluable copyeditor.

I am grateful for the community where I live that Dan Foley, Gene Farley, and Vince Shafer, all fishermen, and Phil Riddle, a former fisherman, mentioned aspects of Pacific fishing, which helped provide details about the industry. We talked as we met at the post office, the dock, or some other location in our small community. Dan read an early version of the trawling chapter and offered corrections relevant to trawling. Vince was fishing out of Newport in those days and remembered hearing about the incident. Greg Streveler helped me understand the currents of the North Pacific.

Dave and Joann Lesh, owners of the Gustavus Inn, gave me the use of two rooms one April as they prepared to open for the summer season. I laid the entire manuscript on the floor, page by page. I crawled around on my hands and knees reading it, moving pages and sections from one spot to another.

My thanks to my husband, Rob Giese, for his support for my writing—he cleans, shovels snow, loads the wood box, buys groceries, does the dishes and other myriad daily living tasks I think I'll do later when I'm finished writing for the day. He also makes sure I go for walks in the woods or on the beach at both ends of the day. He rubs my computer-tired shoulders each morning when he gets up and passes my desk, reading over my shoulder, and for this book, he offered helpful editorial and military suggestions as he paused, sometimes also editing my writing to improve my comments on a man's thoughts or words.

Mary and Bill Schreiber tried to help me locate Dick Cooley's son, Will, called Billy as a boy, but there were no leads solid enough to find him…until the afternoon I sat in the lounge at Seattle's airport waiting for my flight to Oslo, Norway for a different project. Will had ended up at Lorraine Vandecoevering's house. To Lorraine and me, it was a chance fortuitous event. For Will, it was intentional—he was looking for pieces of his life. I had an e-mail from Will Cooley: I hear you've been looking for me. I closed my computer and called him to hang up only as I approached the plane's door. I also spent many hours trying to locate William Clayton but was not so lucky there.

Every book I write has its theme music. I don't know why I choose what I do. While writing this one I listened to three, hundreds of times each—Ennio Mariconi's "The Mission," "The Rough Guide to South African Gospel," and Karl Pearson's "The Armed Man, A Mass for Peace." When I felt stuck, I just put on one of those three, and proceeded with caution.

As always, my kindest thanks to Christopher Robbins, the editor for my first two novels, and now a dear friend who continues to provide strong encouragement.

Ray Shultz told me his margin for error was "this," as he held his thumb and forefinger tips together. Unfortunately, an author's margin for error is greater. While I hope all information is accurate, any errors remain mine alone. I ask the person's forgiveness if I made an error or omitted a public thanks to anyone.

Abigail B. Calkin

December 2011